God Made Them Great

PRESENTED TO

MORVEN CLARK

From

EDDERTON SUNDAY SCHOOL

27th JUNE, 1982.

God Made Them Great

John Tallach

Illustrated by
Lawrence Littleton Evans

THE BANNER OF TRUTH TRUST

THE BANNER OF TRUTH TRUST
The Grey House, 3 Murrayfield Road, Edinburgh EH12 6EL
P.O. Box 621, Carlisle, Pennsylvania 17013, U.S.A.

★

© *John Tallach* 1974
First published 1974
Reprinted with revision 1975
Reprinted 1978
ISBN 0 85151 190 2

★

*Set in 12 on 14 pt. Monotype Bembo
and printed in Great Britain by
Robert MacLehose and Company Limited
Printers to the University of Glasgow*

Preface

Except ye be converted, and become as little children, ye shall not enter into the kingdom of heaven. MATTHEW 18 : 3

These words were spoken by the Lord Jesus. His disciples had just come to Him, asking this question: 'Who is the greatest in the kingdom of heaven?' Without saying anything, Jesus 'called a little child unto him, and set him in the midst of them'. Then He replied, 'Except ye be converted, and become as little children, ye shall not enter into the kingdom of heaven.' How strange – Jesus set this little child as an example before His disciples! He told them to follow the example of a child. But why? Of course Jesus was not telling His disciples that they must stop being grown up, that they must become childish again. Rather, He was telling them this:

The Christian life is not one in which we trust in our own strength, looking after ourselves. On the contrary, it is a life of dependence on God, a life *like* that of the little child who depends on his parents for everything. So Jesus was saying that unless we become child-like in humble dependence on God we cannot 'enter into the kingdom of heaven'.

The following is an account of five Christians who were great in different ways. They came from different countries, and they lived at different times. Yes, they were different, but the reason for their greatness is the same. They were each 'like little children'.

The book is written with the young in view, but I hope that older readers may find it profitable too. Whatever the age of the reader, may God use it to show to all the simplicity of true religion.

September 1973   JOHN TALLACH

Contents

CONTENTS

GEORGE MÜLLER

1 *A rascal changed*

GEORGE was not yet ten years old. His father, a collector of excise money, had left him in a room alone – alone, that is, except for a pile of money.

George waited and watched. Then, in a moment, he had crossed the room and stuffed some of the money into his shoe. He re-crossed the room and sat down.

The door opened, and his father entered. He, too, was interested in that sum of money. He strode over and swiftly counted it.

'Ah! money is missing. Stand up, boy.' Pale-faced, George stood up. His father searched him. Knowing George, he searched him thoroughly, and found the money in his shoe.

George's father had been missing little sums of money for a while. He had left George alone with money just to see if he were the culprit. Now he knew.

George Müller was like that. He learned to steal and cheat at a very early age. He had been born on 27th September, 1805, in Kroppenstadt, Prussia. His parents had been kind to him, but he was soon a heart-break to them.

When George was a little older, he left home to attend a good school in Halberstadt. He was very young to leave home, but I suppose he was quite glad to be away from his father's watchful eye.

When he was fourteen, he returned to his lodgings one evening to find his father waiting for him. 'What is father doing here in Halberstadt?' thought George. He soon knew. George's mother had died and his father had come to take him home to the funeral.

What a sad scene – a young boy following the remains of his mother to the grave, having been such a selfish and disobedient son! But George was not long affected by the shock of his mother's death. He soon showed that he was as sinful and selfish as ever.

With his sixteenth birthday past, George set off on a tour. Where did he find the money? George did not think he needed much money. His plan was to stay in hotels for short whiles, and run away before he was asked for payment.

Having seen Magdeburg and Brunswick, George arrived at Wolfenbüttel, and stayed for two days at an inn. As soon as he arrived, he was on the look-out for a way of escape. He thought of climbing out of the window of his room in the middle of the night, but the window was too high above the ground. There was nothing for it but to make his escape in broad daylight. He walked a little, then ran. But George was suspected, caught, and brought back. He confessed that he had no money, and asked for mercy. But all the mercy he got was to be marched along between two soldiers to stand before a police officer. He was then sent to jail. How George must have fretted, as the festivities of the New Year Season passed while he was locked in a tiny room! Half of January 1822 had passed before his father sent enough money to have him released from prison.

George then went back to his studies, and worked hard, though he continued to live a very sinful life. There was one special reason why he was now spending so much time working. He was preparing to be a clergyman, and he could not hope to get a position with good pay unless he was well trained. Of course the thought did occur to him, that he would need to change his own life if he was going to preach to others. However, George at this stage never went farther than *thinking* about that; he continued for the present to live in the way he had always done.

In a tavern one day, Müller met an old school friend called Beta. They became friends again, and after some months Beta told George that he usually went on Saturday evenings to a Bible-meeting in another friend's house. To Beta's surprise, George became very interested in these meetings, and asked if he could attend one. In the end, Beta agreed. They met one Saturday and went along to Beta's friend's house. Beta's friend was a tradesman called Wagner. The two young men were warmly welcomed at the door and Müller was assured, 'house and heart are open to

you'. Impressed by the welcome afforded to him as a stranger, George's interest increased.

What took place that evening was simple enough, but it proved to be the turning-point in Müller's life. There was singing, reading, and prayer. It was the prayers which most reached Müller's heart. First a man prayed who was afterwards to become a missionary in Africa, but the prayer at the end impressed Müller even more. It was offered by the host himself, and as Müller listened he thought. He was more learned than this man, yet this man could pray so much better than he. Müller listened, and as he listened he began to feel very small. He felt that it was wrong to live a life so empty and sinful as his was. Here was a simple man, but there was so much more in his prayer than in all the sinful pleasures which filled up Müller's life. Wagner's prayer was to Müller like a voice from a world he did not know. It was like a voice from heaven, and Müller's heart was drawn heavenward by it. He left Wagner's house that evening a different man – a man who knew happiness for the first time in his life.

2 *A difficult decision*

GEORGE MÜLLER was now a new man. He was living a new life, a life which he shared with new friends. One of these friends was called Hermann Ball. He had been brought up in a wealthy home, but had given up all his comforts to go to tell the Jews of Poland about Jesus, the only Saviour of sinners. Hermann's example impressed George; he wanted to become a missionary too.

To become a missionary, George would require proper training. But to be allowed to enter a Missionary College he would require to have his father's signature on the form of application. Here was a difficulty. George knew that his father would not be pleased at his plan to become a missionary. Still, he would make the effort, so off he went home by carriage, with the all-important form in his pocket.

George should have enjoyed his supper that evening, but he was thinking too much about what he had come home for.

After supper, George and his father withdrew together to the parlour. There George laid the form before his father. The reply was definite enough:

'I say "No". I mean "No".'

George could not understand his father's attitude at first, but later it became clear. His father had wanted George to become a clergyman, to be well paid, to have an attractive home. This he wanted so that he could come in his old age to share the comforts of his son's home. If George became a missionary, there would be no home for his father to retire to.

That interview must have shaken George. He was being asked to think of his father, instead of giving his life to God. He thought about the choice very deeply, and then he came to a decision. If his father was going to come between him and serving God, he would have to live without his father's help. He would take no more money from him as long as he lived.

Back at University in Halle, George became more and more aware of what he had done. He had cut himself off from his only source of support. What could he do now? One morning, at breakfast-time, he knew what he would do. He went on his knees, told his needs to God, and asked for His help.

Later, George heard a knock at the door of his room. One of his tutors stood there. He was not alone: he had an American visitor with him. George welcomed both men, and closed the door. But the men had no time to chat; they had come for a special purpose. This American wished to learn German. George's tutor had brought the visitor along to arrange with George to teach him German. There would in fact be several men whom he would teach. They would study together, and would pay George separately for his help. Only then did George realize what this unexpected visit meant. It meant that he would have money to help him pay the expenses his father used to pay for him. More than that, it meant that God had immediately answered his prayer for help.

[7]

Later that year, George became very concerned about where he should go as a missionary. He had hoped to go to Bucharest, but war broke out in that area, and he was prevented. One day, during that time when George was praying for guidance, he had a meal with the tutor already mentioned. This man had a suggestion to make. He wanted George to apply to a society in London which sent out missionaries to the Jews. After praying about this George agreed, and Dr Tholuck sent off an application for him. For a long time, George waited. At last one reply came, and, months afterwards, another. At last he knew he had been accepted as a missionary to the Jews.

There were difficulties, however. George would have to go to London, and he would have to study with the Society for six months before they sent him out as a missionary. Reluctantly, George accepted this delay and sailed for London in March, 1829. There he studied for twelve hours each day, but all the time his thoughts were flitting away from Hebrew Grammar to the Jews in Houndsditch and Hyde Park. George longed to go out and tell them about his Saviour, instead of sitting at his books all day.

After two months of study, George became ill. His doctor sent him to recover in the fresh sea air of Devon. In the quietness and peace of Teignmouth, the future missionary benefited in body and in soul. When he returned to London in September 1829, he was like a new man. He began a prayer-meeting among fellow students from six to eight each morning: in the evening too, he often held family prayers. Apart from that, George often spent hours in prayer alone. But this was not the only direction in which George's new zeal moved him. He became convinced that he should add practical work to his studies. He began preaching on a street corner in the Jewish community, and gathered together fifty boys to whom he would read the Scriptures.

Late in December, George was back in Devon. The sea was a great attraction: he used to love watching it stretch out till it merged with the sky. The sea was free, thought George, but he was not. He was hemmed in, he was restricted, up in London. Then he decided. He would leave London and come down to Devon. He would also leave the Mission Society, and would from now on work on his own. So he left London, came down to the little fishing village of Teignmouth, and began to preach there. A small congregation soon asked him to become their minister, and George accepted the invitation. Of course although he was now a minister in Teignmouth, he was free to preach elsewhere at times.

One other place where George sometimes preached was quite a distance away, in Exeter. However the distance was no obstacle, and George was soon very keen to make that particular journey. He had met a lady there whom he had admired at once. She was so honest. He had given up a pretty girl in Germany, and this English lady was eight years older than himself, but George knew where his heart lay. In October, 1830, he married Mary Groves.

3 Beginnings at Bristol

GEORGE MÜLLER had known Henry Craik for some time now. He had come to know him in Teignmouth. The two were about the same age, and held the same beliefs, though they were very different men. In February, 1832, Henry lost his young wife, and he was soon prevailed on to go to Bristol for a time. There was a congregation there without a pastor, and he had been asked to preach there.

Soon after Henry arrived in Bristol, a thought occurred to him. There was so much need in the city, so much work to be done – wouldn't it be fine if George would leave Teignmouth and join him?

Poor Mary Müller! She was probably by now quite attached to their home in Teignmouth, and she was looking forward to having her first child in September. Now she was being asked to leave her pleasant sea-side home and settle in the middle of a dirty, noisy city. But she knew one thing. Neither her husband nor Henry Craik had made up their minds to change to Bristol without praying for three weeks for guidance. She knew her duty was to believe and obey.

So the two country pastors came to settle in Bristol towards the end of May. Things were not easy for them that summer. Cholera broke out, and many of the people of Bristol died. In August the heat became unbearable. The heat and the plague! The two young ministers seemed to have been called to serve in a city of sick and dying. September came, but no deliverance: still death stalked the streets. No doubt the temptation was there, to forget the suffering that surrounded them. No doubt George sometimes felt that he should stay at home, that he should care for his wife. Perhaps if he went on like this the child she was expecting would never know its father. But then the doleful tolling of the funeral bell would sound again, and George would again resolve: as long as he had strength he must go about those streets.

Then, in October, the plague that had caused the death of many began itself to die. No wonder we read of a day set apart for thanksgiving! And now there was time for George to rest a little. Time to hear the tiny cry that made such a change from the funeral bell. Time to take up the little bundle of life, born in the shadow of the deadly plague: baby Lydia Müller.

4 *How far can a shilling go?*

JUST after New Year's Day, 1833, a special letter arrived at Mr Müller's home. It had come from Bagdad. £200 the envelope contained, and the letter invited George and Henry to leave immediately as missionaries to Bagdad.

For the last few years, George had always had a desire to sail off to some strange foreign country with the gospel. As he trudged the dirty, slushy streets of Bristol these January days, this call to Bagdad had a special appeal.

But something kept Müller from going to Bagdad – he could not forget the needs of Bristol. In fact, once he had put Bagdad out of his mind, the needs of those around him came more into his mind than ever before.

He was specially concerned about orphans in slum areas. Many of these children were kept in large unfriendly almshouses, which they shared with criminals and lunatics.

Müller heard about societies which ran free day schools for slum children, and for a time he contributed to their support. But he became concerned about the way these schools were run. For one thing, if a man gave money to support the schools, he had a say in how the schools should be run, whether he was a Christian or not. By the beginning of 1834, George had made up his mind on the matter. He felt that God was directing him to begin an organisation which would include the provision of day schools for slum children. It would be called the 'Scriptural Knowledge Institution'. The Institution would also run Sabbath Schools, would help to distribute Bibles, and would provide support for missionaries.

It was a lot of work to undertake, and Müller's wife told him so.

The proposed increase of George's responsibilities came at an awkward time. They had in fact one shilling in the home at the time George spoke about it. Mary wondered how far a shilling would go to provide for themselves alone, far less for themselves plus George's new projects. Also, another little mouth would soon need to be fed.

Müller's son was born on the 19th March. For a time, his new plans were somewhat elbowed out of his thoughts. Then, in April, he came right back to thinking about them. He prayed, and said that, if he didn't get money soon he'd have to give up his plans. He added that, if he got twenty pounds, he would use it to start his new work. He would use it to buy Bibles, and give them away.

That same day, a woman came to the Müllers' home and handed George an envelope. It contained twenty pounds.

'Madam, do you want me to spend this for something special?' George asked.

'Well – what I had in mind was – Bibles'.

That was the beginning, and the work grew until a school became established – a school which was thoroughly Christian.

Then the school's headmaster told Mr Müller about something which disturbed him. If pupils who attended the school became orphans, they were taken from the school and placed in the horrible almshouses. There they remained until considered old enough (they were still very young) to work. George said he wanted to do something to prevent this happening. The head-master replied that the almshouses provided food for the children – the school could not care for the orphans in this way.

Müller had his answer – 'We'll teach the children in orphanages instead of schools.' (In 1835, orphanages were almost unheard of in any part of the country.) The headmaster was not encouraging: 'You don't have the time. You're the pastor of a church. You have the day school already. And if you'll pardon me for saying this, Mr Müller, you don't have the money either'.

The headmaster seemed to be speaking the truth. Müller's idea now looked silly. But he wanted to know one thing, before he ruled out the possibility of beginning an orphanage. Why had the thought of an orphanage occurred to him? had not God put the thought into his mind? If he knew that this was God's plan, then was not He the God of the impossible?

5 A voice from the past

FOR a month, George thought about it. Then Mary's brother came home. He was a dentist, and a missionary in the East Indies. He was going on to Germany to encourage others to join him in mission work, and he asked George to go as interpreter. The journey took a long time in those days. But it was a chance to think, an opportunity to pray.

When George and his brother-in-law arrived in Halle, George looked up his former tutor – the one who had advised him to go to London. Then a simple thing happened – simple but significant. George asked Dr Tholuck for the address of a mutual friend. He was told that he stayed in a building used as an orphanage. In fact George himself had stayed in a room in this orphanage when he had been a student in Halle.

The orphanage had been built over a hundred years before by a man called Francke. George had often thought of this before, but the fact came to him with increased force now: Francke had built this orphanage before 1727 by faith and prayer alone. He had asked no man for any funds. He had asked in secret, and his

GOD MADE THEM GREAT

Heavenly Father had rewarded him openly. George wondered as he stood again within the precincts of this ancient house. Had God taken him from England just to show him over a house that proved His power to answer prayer?

In six weeks, he was home again. Still turning things over in his mind, he went about his duties as a pastor. One evening he went to have tea with a Christian lady, but more than his tea was awaiting him in her home, for while there he once more came across the biography of Francke of Halle. The effect was so much the greater, as Müller had so recently seen the Orphan Homes Francke had built by faith. The next day, and for days after that, a voice seemed to say to Müller: 'You should do the same'. Not, of course, just to imitate A. H. Francke, but Müller's motive was this:

Many times he met believers who were afflicted by doubts. They knew that the Bible was true, they had heard of many proofs of it in the past, but still they had doubts. Müller wanted to prove to them that God was still as true to His word as He had been in the past. If God would provide an orphanage in answer to faith and prayer, would that not encourage the people of God to believe?

For weeks he prayed. Each day, it was the same prayer. He needed a thousand pounds to start this work. Also, he needed a suitable house, three or four of a staff, and all the different things that a house needs. One day, he was thinking about this prayer of his. Was he asking for too much? He opened his Bible and began to read at Psalm 79. He read through Psalm 80 to Psalm 81. He came to verse 10: 'Open thy mouth wide and I will fill it'. Surely this was God's voice! Others had said that he was mad, but not God. God had surely told him to go on.

Five days later Müller was reading out to his wife the contents of a letter received from a Christian couple. It read:

'We propose ourselves for the intended Orphan House, if you think us qualified for it; also to give up all the furniture which the Lord has given us for the use of your home, and to do this without receiving any salary whatever, believing that if it be the will of the Lord to employ us, He will supply our needs'.

On the day that Müller received this letter, another woman offered her services as well for the Orphan House, and yet another woman gave ten shillings towards it. About the same time he received £100 from a poor seamstress who earned about 3s. 6d. per week. Müller was so surprised that he decided to call on this lady. She explained that she had inherited the money and said, 'Rather than the Orphan Home should not be established, I will give all the money I have'. Still afraid that she might be offering the money rashly, Müller asked if she had counted the cost. What could he answer when she replied: 'The Lord Jesus has given His last drop of blood for me, and should I not give Him this £100?'

Apart from such gifts of money there were also handed over plates, basins, jugs, mugs, knives, forks, and a blanket.

The climax to these encouragements came at the end of January, 1836. George rushed home to tell Mary about it. Number 6 Wilson Street was now theirs, to be used as an Orphan House.

6 Trials begin

FEBRUARY 3rd was just another working day for most of the citizens of Bristol, though they may have have been cheered in their daily routine by the sight of the odd spring snowdrop. But on that day Müller was not looking to the new life beginning to brighten the grimy city gardens. He was thinking of another kind of beginning. In a sense, today was the day for the life of the

[15]

Orphanage to begin: it was the day appointed for receiving applications.

But, by lunch time, no one had applied to have any orphan children received. 'Perhaps in the afternoon', thought Müller. But the clock in No 6 Wilson Street ticked its way through all the hours of afternoon and still the report was the same: 'No applications received'.

That evening Müller felt very low. Perhaps, after all his praying and all his trusting, God was not in this at all. He humbled himself before God and searched his heart. Then suddenly he stumbled on the truth. Everything they had prayed for they had received. But they had not prayed for children. No wonder that none had turned up! It was God's gentle reminder that they were engaged in His work, and not their own, so throughout the evening of February 3rd, 1836, George committed the whole matter to the Lord. The next day, the first application for admission was received and it was not long before the house was full.

After that, things went easily for a time. In eight months, another house on Wilson Street had been taken over for infant orphans. Nine months later again, a third house was opened for thirty orphan boys.

Then came a period of trial. On August 18th, 1838, for example, Müller confesses, 'I have not one penny in hand for the orphans. In a day or two again many pounds will be needed'. During these months, God supplied Muller's needs day by day, rather than month by month. Sometimes it was hour by hour. Time and again he had to pray to God: 'We need so much by such a time – if we do not get it, we must close'. And the money always came, without Müller's breathing a hint of his needs to any man. Such an instance occurred in February, 1842. One day he wrote: 'If the Lord were not to send means by nine o'clock tomorrow morning, His name would be dishonoured. But I am fully assured that He will not leave us'.

By seven o'clock the next morning, Müller's expectation had

not been fulfilled. At that time there was a business-man walking along to work. He thought for a moment of the orphans, and decided he would call in the evening with some money. He went on. Then he felt somehow he must go immediately with his gift, so he turned back along the street. As he retraced his steps, it came forcibly to his mind that important matters had to be dealt with at his office, so again he came to a stand. He felt he must go to his work, and yet he could not. He did not know it, but God's honour was at stake – He must justify George Müller's trust in Him. So the thought kept hammering at the business-man's brain: 'Go at once, go at once'. In the end he surrendered, turned again towards the orphanage, and handed in three sovereigns.

About the same time, things got so bad that Müller had to tell his staff the difficulty they were in. He had long held back from telling them, because he had said at the beginning he would make known his needs to God alone. But now he saw that his own staff members were different. It was not breaking his rule to tell *them* how things stood. They were all Christians, engaged in the same work as himself. It was right that they should share the burden of prayer with him, though no one else would be told.

Müller was deeply moved by their response. The cook gave the six pounds which she had lodged in the bank. Another woman refused to take her salary, saying her widow's pension was quite enough.

But the small pile of coins which his willing staff had collected disappeared by the end of the week. Müller had to call them together again to ask them to pray. After a time, someone handed over a small collection. He asked where it had come from, but no one would say. He demanded to know. Then his helpers confessed that they had sold off little articles in their possession. They had felt they could not heartily pray to God for help while they knew they themselves kept back some unnecessary things.

But in a day or two, this money was spent as well. Then Müller wrote: 'The funds are exhausted'. The Orphan Houses stood stripped of all articles that could be parted with, and Müller had no money in his hand. It looked like the end.

7 Number 4

A WOMAN passed down Wilson Street and stared in at the front window of Number 6. Then she entered, bringing a huge bag with her. She asked to see Mr Müller.

When she caught sight of the director of the Orphanage, she began to chat with him in an excited way about Bristol. It was such a pleasant change from London, and so on. Müller must have sighed. What had this talkative woman to do with him, or with the answer to his prayers which he hourly offered up? He soon knew.

She emptied her purse on the table. The money came to £3 2s. 6d. George's heart missed a beat. Then this lady told him she had been lodging next door for the past five days. She had not called sooner with the money because they had seemed so busy in the Orphanage. These five days had been among the most trying in Müller's life. The money he needed had lain next door until his need was desperate.

£3 2s. 6d. would not go far. But the whole experience went a long way towards confirming Müller's faith. Now he saw it clearly: 'It was from the beginning in the heart of God to help us, but because He delights in the prayers of His children, He allowed us to pray so long; also to try our faith, and to make the answer so much the sweeter'.

In October, 1842, another lady spoke to Müller about five hundred pounds which she had recently inherited. She wanted him to pray that she would be guided to spend it on the right thing. For a time Müller prayed that this lady would be made so happy in the Saviour whom she followed that she would be willing to use her money to support His cause. Then, in December, he heard that she had finally decided to give money to help run his Orphanage. There was a big bill due in January so Müller was very relieved at the news.

However, January arrived and no money had come through: some difficulty had arisen about transferring it. So the lady's money could not be used to settle the big account after all. It was settled some other way.

Only in March did he hear again from her. Five hundred pounds was now waiting for him at his local bank, to be used as he saw fit. It was a colossal sum. There was enough in it to pay expenses in the three homes for more than a year. The work had never been so well off.

Just at this time, the housemother in 6 Wilson Street asked to see Mr Müller. She wanted to speak about 4 Wilson Street. Müller thought the children had been up to mischief again, but it was nothing like that. The Grahams in Number 4 were going to leave, and had given first offer of the house to the Orphanage. The housemother had thanked Mr Graham, but told him his house was out of the question for the Orphanage.

Müller, however, was not so sure. A number of applications had been made in recent weeks which he had not been able to receive for lack of room. Also two Christian ladies had just been asking him if he had work for them at the Orphanage. Again, would it not show the world that he did not regret beginning this work of faith if he expanded it now, in spite of these years of difficulty? And of course, there was the widow's five hundred pounds.

[19]

But even all this was not everything to George Müller. No matter how right a step appeared to be, he never took it without prayer. So for the next weeks, as he went about his work, he was constantly seeking confirmation of God's will. Then something occurred to him. He had been given an opportunity to expand the work, in dependence on God. What if he did not expand? People would say that he had lost his faith. They would say that George Müller had spent long enough living by faith – now he was afraid.

That decided him. Next day he called at Number 4. Mr Graham did not welcome him. In the interval, he told his visitor, he had changed his mind – he wasn't going to move now. Müller asked hopefully if Mr Graham were going to look at all further for a new house. He was told that there was one week left before he had to make up his mind definitely.

Throughout that week Müller prayed that God would find a place for the Graham family, so that Number 4 would become available. When the week had passed, he found himself again at the front door of Number 4. Mr Graham was in a different mood this time. He welcomed George in. But Müller only wanted to know one thing – were the Grahams going to leave or not? The answer was – 'Yes, and as soon as possible.' That summer, Number 4 Wilson Street became the fourth Orphan House in Bristol which had been provided by faith and prayer.

8 *Exodus*

GEORGE MÜLLER was getting to be a big spender. Of course he did not spend the money he was given on himself. He spent it carefully and prayerfully, supporting the cause of his Lord in different ways. But however much money he was given, he did not hoard it up.

That is why he had not till now built an Orphan House. Building a house requires a huge sum of money, so Müller had rented instead the houses in Wilson Street. The plan to build an orphanage came in a rather roundabout way.

It all began with a letter Müller got on October 30th, 1845. That was a Thursday, and he was so caught up with other things that he could hardly take in its contents at the time. But the letter was always at the back of his mind, and by Monday morning he had to take several hours to pray over the matter before God. The letter was from a man in Wilson Street, and though he wrote in a friendly way there could be no doubt that the letter was really a complaint. The people of Wilson Street were being disturbed by the noise. In other ways, too, they found it difficult to share a street with scores of lively children. As to whether or not Müller should take his orphans elsewhere, the writer left it to the Master of the Homes to decide.

I suppose Müller would have liked to be able to burn the letter and forget about it. But he could not forget it. It seemed to him, though he knew the Lord had provided homes for these children in Wilson Street, that this neighbour did have some ground for complaint. And something else entered Müller's thoughts as well.

Perhaps he *ought* to move – perhaps the *Lord* meant him to. He drew up reasons. There was no room for children to play in Wilson Street. There was no land for cultivation. The houses were too confined – there was no room in these houses for a special place to nurse sick children. Also, the homes were in a slum area – might it not be better for the children to be taken out of such circumstances altogether and placed in a healthier situation? As Müller thought the letter over, he concluded – 'Yes, it *is* God's voice.'

So he prayed his boldest prayer yet. In his prayer he mentioned that the homes would have to close, or be placed elsewhere in the slums, or else he would have to build new homes on an open piece of ground. He asked that, if it were God's will, he would find a piece of land seven acres in size, so that he could build a place for about three hundred children. He also asked for ten thousand pounds.

Morning and evening George prayed that prayer. He prayed it for thirty-six days. Then on December 10, 1845, another letter arrived. It was so different from the one sent by the Wilson Street man. George knew now surely that it was God's will for him to build a new orphanage altogether. This letter contained a gift of one thousand pounds – the largest that he had ever received.

A few days later, Mary's sister came down to Bristol from London. And she had news. A London architect had heard of Müller's work among orphans. When Mary's sister told him that George was going to build an orphanage, he said he would superintend the building without making any charge.

After that, things moved slowly for a time. Then, early in 1846, George heard about land for sale on Ashley Down. He went up to see it. It was on a hill, just outside Bristol, and there were seven acres of it. It was exactly what he had been looking for.

The next day, he went to see the owner of Ashley Down. He was not at home. Determined to find him, Müller went to his place of business. But he was not there either – he had just left for home. Puzzled, Müller debated. In the end, he decided not to follow the man back to his home; there must be some reason why he had missed him at both places.

So he went home, and all evening he felt he had done the right thing. I suppose George slept well that night – he had done so much walking these days! But the land-owner did not. He lay awake from 3 till 5 a.m. He was thinking about his land, and a voice seemed to say to him, 'Sell Ashley Down to George Müller'. So he decided he would. But that was not all he decided before the clock struck five that February morning. He would give

Müller the land for an orphanage, and, more than that, he would sell at £120 an acre, instead of £200. This was the news awaiting George, when he found the businessman early at his desk next day. It was welcome news, for he could easily manage £840. At the selling-rate of the previous day, he could not have bought the ground.

Now Müller had a piece of land, and an architect to plan the building. At the end of the year, he had received over six thousand pounds to finance the building. Less than three years after that, the complete new Orphanage on Ashley Down stood ready to receive its orphans. Every bill had been paid, and there were seven hundred pounds still in the bank.

So from June 18th to 21st, 1849, all the children from the Wilson Street Homes were busy packing their little bags. In batches, they lined up outside the old Orphanage and began their march to the new one. Out of the slums they marched, and on till

Bristol itself was almost left behind. Then they began to climb. They struggled up the rise till their massive new home loomed up before them.

What a place! Three hundred children it would take – one hundred and twenty from Wilson Street, the rest straight from the Bristol slums. As George and Mary watched them file through the doorway, their hearts sang the praises of the One with whom 'nothing shall be impossible.'

9 *Boiler trouble*

B UT a year and a half after he and Mary had watched the orphans filing up the hill to Ashley Down, Müller began to think again about expansion. Why stop at three hundred orphans— why not go on to a thousand?

Others tried to dissuade him: they said he had reached his limit. But people didn't need to talk to George Müller about reaching a limit. He knew that to set a limit to a work of God was to set a limit to God Himself. That, George Müller refused to do.

George made up his mind quite quickly, though he kept his decision to himself for a time. He *would* provide a home for a thousand orphans. As proof of his intentions, he began to ask for applications to fill up the places in the expanded Orphanage. It was not long before he had a list containing three hundred and fifty names.

He had the names of plenty of orphan children, but he was receiving very little money to help put a roof over their heads.

Once or twice a good donation came in, but for the most part there was very little. However, the word of God sustained him: he was thinking a lot of what was said about Abraham, 'After he had patiently endured, he obtained the promise' (Hebrews 6 : 15). After many months, the same God as had supported the work with sixpences and shillings moved several Christians to donate together £5,700. Surely this was a God who knew no limits at all!

March, 1855, saw Müller and a Bristol land agent together on Ashley Down. George was asking about a piece of land to the north-east of the Orphanage already built. But the agent shook his head – the land was not for sale. George had had his eye on that piece of land for years, only to find that it wasn't for sale! He would see the owner, he told the land agent. But he couldn't do that, he was told; the owner was dead! George was cornered for a moment. The owner had left in his will that the land could not be leased or sold for a hundred years. Suddenly Müller shot off from the land agent's side. 'Where is he going – why should he vent his annoyance on me?' the agent thought. But Müller was not a man to spend energy merely on getting angry. He was pacing, now this way, now that, in front of the Orphanage. He counted two hundred yards to this side, two hundred yards to that. With an exclamation of satisfaction, he told the agent that he no longer required his services. He would build his new orphanage in two parts on his own land, one on each side of the existing building!

Müller had known beforehand that this new project would cost £35,000. Yet he had believed that his plans would materialise. By March, 1862, the two new buildings were finished. And he had received, for this work alone, not £35,000, but £46,000. Now Müller had a thousand children of all ages who depended on him for a home, for every stitch they wore, and every scrap they ate.

★

While Müller had patiently waited during these years for money, his faith had been tried in other ways as well. Just as the 1857 winter was coming on, for example, the big boiler in one of the Orphan Houses began to leak. This was the only source of heating for the whole house, so Müller began to fear that his children would have to endure a lot of cold. He went down to the boiler house. The boiler itself was not easy to get at; it was cased in a wall of bricks. Even to get behind this wall would take some time, Müller thought. To replace the boiler altogether, of course, would take weeks.

Müller was distressed to think of the children in their huge home with no heating, but he knew the boiler must be looked at before the weather got even colder than it was. So, asking God to help him, he arranged with workmen to call on a certain day.

As if to make matters worse, a cold north wind blew up, and all Bristol began to shiver. The night before the workmen were due, that bleak north wind still blew, but Müller did not tell the men to wait for warmer weather. He had already asked God for that, and had added the prayer that the workmen would be made willing to work hard, so that the boiler would not be out of use for long.

During the night, the north wind died away. In the morning, a warm wind blew from the south. The weather was so mild that no fire was needed at all, even though it was December.

The boiler-men worked all day. At half-past eight at night Müller was on his way home when he was told the workmen's boss had arrived. He turned back, and went downstairs to meet this man. He was telling Müller that his men would work late that night, and return early the next morning, when the men straightened their backs and spoke for themselves. Were they refusing to do overtime? On the contrary, they told their boss they would work all night! Müller's prayers were now fully answered, and the fire was lit again in the Orphanage boiler by lunch time of the next day.

10 *Into all the world*

THE work of the Orphanage went on as usual for the next three years, until George was handed five thousand pounds. Of course he began to think, 'Why only one thousand – why not two thousand orphans?'

By January 6th, 1870, it was more than a thought – it was an accomplished fact. Now Ashley Down housed a small township of two thousand boys and girls. It was wonderful that Mary lived to see that day, for she did not live to see many more. It was only a month later that she died.

As Müller thought back over their life together, he felt his loss to be unspeakable. How precious it was to him that they had been given 'twelve months of happiness in the year, and thus, year after year.' Yet he conducted the funeral service himself, showing that, in the midst of his loss, his faith in God was still the same. During his address on the words, 'Thou art good and doest good' (Psalm 119 : 68) George said that, if it were the easiest thing in the world to bring his wife back again he would not do it. 'God Himself has done it,' he said. 'We are satisfied with Him.'

When Mary died, Müller was almost sixty-five years old. This is the age at which most men retire, but George Müller's most active years were yet to come. It was only now that he thought of travelling from land to land, testifying to God's mercy and faithfulness to him. Müller travelled two hundred thousand miles, through forty-two different countries. He preached to three million people. Of course many interesting things happened to him, even during these closing years of his life, but there is only room here for one of them.

On one of his voyages to America, Müller's ship was off Newfoundland when a very thick fog came down. The Captain ordered speed to be reduced. The ship went more and more slowly, till she hardly moved at all.

The captain was worried; he remained on the bridge himself for twenty-two hours on end. Suddenly he was startled by a tap on the shoulder. He turned round to see George Müller of Bristol.

'Captain', he said, 'I have come to tell you that I must be in Quebec on Saturday afternoon.' This was Wednesday.

'It's impossible.'

'Very well, if your ship cannot take me, God will find some other means of locomotion to take me. I have never broken an engagement in fifty-seven years.'

The Captain protested that it was beyond his power to be of any assistance – what *could* be done?

'Let us go down to the chart room and pray', Müller suggested.

The Captain looked at the stranger on the bridge and wondered if he were mad.

'Do you know how dense this fog is?'

'No', said Müller, 'my eye is not on the density of the fog, but on the living God, who controls every circumstance of my life.'

Müller then acted on what he had just said, going on his knees to offer a simple prayer. In his prayer he asked that, if it were God's will, He would take the fog away in five minutes.

The Captain thought to himself: 'That would suit a children's class, where the children were not more than eight or nine years of age.'

Then his visitor was standing again, and the Captain thought he had better begin a prayer himself. But Müller stopped him.

'First, you do not believe God will do it. Second, I believe He has done it, and there is no need whatever for you to pray about it. Get up, Captain, and open the door, and you will find the fog is gone.'

The Captain got up and opened the door. The fog *was* gone, and Müller *was* in Quebec that Saturday as he had said.

11 *The 'tomorrow' that never came*

SOMETIME in 1897, an old man took up his pen and began to compile a report. He had written many before, but this was to be his last. At the age of ninety-two, Müller allowed his lively mind to roam back over the sixty-three years since the work had begun.

He had felt so sorry for the children of those Bristol slums. It had been difficult, but he had been determined to provide them with schools. By 1897, he had given 122,683 pupils a Christian education.

Over a quarter of a million Bibles, and almost a million and a half New Testaments had been distributed at home and abroad. Especially was Müller glad to recall how the word of God had been blessed to Roman Catholics in Ireland, Spain and Italy.

For sixty-three years he had been praying for missionaries in many a dark corner of the globe. He had sent them money, too—over a quarter of a million pounds. And it had not been in vain. He felt sure that, through these missionaries, thousands of souls had been brought to know the Lord Jesus.

Of course, these and other aspects of his work had required a constant and increasing supply of money. Where did it all come from? who was to receive the credit for it all? Müller, in looking back, gave no credit to man. When he had faced his many trials and difficulties, he had not looked to man for support. Should he not now give the glory to whom alone it was due, as he reviewed the support he had received?

How much had the Lord given him? One million, four hundred and twenty-four thousand, six hundred and forty-six pounds, six shillings and ninepence halfpenny.

And how his mind lingered over the orphans! Many thousands he had cared for, but there was something more important to Müller than the total figure. One thousand, eight hundred and thirteen children had left his Orphanages declaring their trust to be in Christ alone.

★

George Müller's son-in-law, Jim Wright, was to succeed him in his work. By 1898, the younger man was afraid that Müller was not fit for the amount of work he was doing. On the evening of March 9th, he pleaded with the lively old man to rest more, to stay longer in bed. In fact he asked him to take a longer rest as from the very next morning. Müller's reply was typical: 'We will say nothing about tomorrow.'

The next morning a maid knocked on his bedroom door around seven o'clock and got no reply. Opening the door, she took in his usual cup of tea. But he was gone: George Müller was dead.

The last time he had preached to his own congregation the text had been: 'For we know that if our earthly house of this tabernacle were dissolved, we have a building of God, a house not made with hands, eternal in the heavens.' (II Corinthians 5 : 1) Now Müller knew more about that than he had ever done before.

ISOBEL KUHN

1 *Night of despair*

WHETHER she got them from her father or her mother I do not know, but Isobel Miller came into the world sporting freckles and a tilted nose.

As she grew up she saw life in different American cities – Pittsburgh, Cleveland, Philadelphia, St Louis. Her father's work seemed to take him from one end of America to the other. Sometimes money was scarce in those days at the beginning of this century. With father away from home, mother would then call Isobel and her brother Murray to pray with her for food.

– 'Always the next day a letter would come with enough money to tide us over.'

Things were scarce sometimes, but on the whole Isobel had a happy childhood. When her family at last settled in Vancouver, Canada, she was becoming an attractive little girl. She had bright brown eyes and soft dark hair. She was clever, too; soon she was top of her class in school.

Things looked bright as Isobel grew up, and they stayed that way for a time. At University she was an outstanding and popular girl. Then a shadow came.

She was at an English class, and her professor was talking about the Bible. He said that nobody believed it any more. Then, as an afterthought, he asked if anyone in the class of about a hundred did believe that the Bible was true. Only one hand went up, along with Isobel's. Then came the sneer which Isobel felt so keenly:

'Oh, you just believe that because your papa and your mama told you so.' Isobel had been brought up to respect the Bible, but she had never come to trust in Jesus herself. Now she was further from Him than ever before.

There was another thing, too, which came as a shadow over her young life. She had been friendly with a tall young man for two years now, and was engaged to marry him. However, all her hopes came to a sudden end when she learned that he was taking another girl out behind her back. Isobel felt shattered. Was there any real love in the world at all?

One sleepless night she heard her father enter her bedroom. He knelt beside her bed to pray. When he rose, she said: 'Thanks, Dad, but it doesn't go beyond the ceiling, you know.' She never forgot the groan with which he turned and left the room.

Isobel was getting desperate. She was working hard all day, and having no rest at night. It was December now, around her twentieth birthday. Outside the house, the city of Vancouver lay silent in the darkness. The Post Office clock in Main Street struck two, and she was still turning and tossing in her bed. For Isobel, everything was dark that night: it was the blackest night of her young life. Then, in the midst of the darkness, a thought came to her: 'What's the use of all this misery – I can end it all in a moment'. She got out of bed and went along to the bathroom: there was a bottle there marked 'poison'. With her hand on the door knob she paused: the silence of the night had been broken. Her father lay sleeping in the next room, and his three loud groans startled her into remembrance of him. Her father had been so kind, she thought. How could she repay his kindness like this? It was just enough to restrain her. Back she went to her bedroom and sat in a heap on her bed. She could not escape from life, and yet she could not face it. Then something stirred in her mind. It was the memory of a line of poetry she had been reading: it went like this,

[34]

'In His will is our peace.'

She did not yet believe what the poet said, but what she did say was this: 'What if, after all, there *is* a God? I have certainly not been in His will, and I have certainly had no peace'. Then, in the darkness and loneliness of her bedroom she raised her desperate hands above her head and said: 'God, if there be a God, if You will prove to me that You are, and if You will give me peace, I will give You my whole life. I'll do anything You ask me to do, go where You send me, obey You all my days'. Then she got into bed and slept.

Vancouver city was far advanced with the business of the next day when Isobel's tired body stirred to life. For moments she lay contentedly, basking in the sunshine that streamed through her bedroom window. Then suddenly she thought – 'When did I last sleep like that?' Slowly the events of the early hours drifted back into her memory. Among other things, she recalled her cry to the God who might or might not exist. Then she shook herself. She was not a believer in God, and yet she had to face the truth. She had prayed for peace, and peace had come – surely that was the hand of God? Again she sat on the edge of the bed that had seen her darkest hour the night before. She thought. God did appear to have kept His side – why should she not keep hers and fulfil her promise to seek Him?

This seemed so reasonable that she resolved to begin again to read the Bible she had known as a child. She began praying, too, and received clear answers to her prayers. After that, she could no longer address her prayers 'To God, *if* He existed'. Now she knew.

2 'The Firs' and Mr Fraser

MRS WHIPPLE was plump and cheery. She had been for years a believer in the Lord Jesus Christ, and she wished that others would come to trust Him as she did herself. One of the ways she sought this was to arrange the Firs Conference.

This Bible Conference was held by the shores of the beautiful Lake Whatcom in Washington. It was called the 'Firs Conference' because many fir trees grew around that part. It was in the summer of 1923 that Isobel came here first, but perhaps her most memorable visit was paid the year after that. 1924 was the year that J. O. Fraser was at 'The Firs'.

J. O. Fraser was a wonderful missionary. Isobel learned that he had gone out with the gospel to China years before. But in the end he had become a missionary to a mountain tribe who were not in fact Chinese. They were the Lisu people, and Mr Fraser had only gradually learned of their existence from seeing them occasionally at Chinese markets. Mr Fraser had one great desire, when he came on holiday like this to western countries: he wanted Christians from the homelands to go with him to China to help him bring the gospel to that needy land. Isobel was deeply impressed: yes, she would like to help Mr Fraser in his great work. She was only a girl, but she would like to do her best.

When the Conference broke up, Isobel got a great surprise. Mr Fraser was coming to stay with her family! Her father had been at the Conference too, and had asked him: he was to stay for a week.

They were taking a walk by the beach when she got a chance to ask him about being a missionary. He was not encouraging.

'Missionary life can be very lonely', he said. His blue-grey eyes were scanning the ocean as he said this, and he hardly seemed to be speaking to Isobel at all. He seemed more to speak to himself, and on and on he went, talking of a life that was hard, yet happy. He was looking back on his own life, but he was looking forward, too. Of course Isobel did not know it, but Mr Fraser was describing experiences which would be exactly hers in the years to come.

3 *In training*

CHICAGO was a big dirty city. Isobel hated the dirt and the noise, but she came here all the same in 1924. Only one thing had brought her – the fact that the Moody Bible Institute was there.

She had been teaching in Vancouver, but had given that up to train for her missionary work. Another girl had been preparing to go to China too, but had been prevented. She used her savings to pay for Isobel's first year at Chicago.

Isobel spent two years at the Bible Institute. Sometimes she had to work in cafés to support herself. At other times she was helped by friends. In one way or another she got through, and felt the whole training helpful.

She graduated in December 1926: it was an experience she always remembered. For every graduation, two speakers were chosen, one from the men's side and one from the women's. Isobel had been chosen to represent the women students as she was a first-class speaker. On the big day, however, she met with disappointment: she faltered in the middle of her address. She felt she had let down those who had chosen her, and as soon as she could she ran off to her room to cry. Then the Lord met her in the midst of her weakness and said, 'The beloved of the Lord shall dwell in safety by Him; and the Lord shall cover him all the day long, and he shall dwell between His shoulders' (Deuteronomy 33 : 12). This verse of the Bible was as if spoken to her, and she never forgot it. As she left Chicago now for the next stage of preparation, she was not thinking of herself, she was not even worried about the little failure which had so upset her at the time. She looked to God's glory now, and not her own. Now she looked to Him alone to keep her, and to love her with His changeless love.

Isobel was now fully accepted as a missionary to China, but for the moment it was not possible for her to go. Sometimes it was difficult for foreigners to get entrance into China; this must have been one of those times. As she waited in Vancouver, she was not idle. She was doing useful work in the Lord's service among the office girls of the city.

She had plenty to think about too – for one thing, she thought of getting married! She had become friendly with a young man at the Bible College in Chicago, and now she knew by his letters that he wished her to be his wife. He had gone off to China already, in 1926, but she would soon be following him. Isobel loved John Kuhn, but she had a problem. John was interested in work in Kansu, a province of north-west China. For her part, ever since hearing Mr Fraser speak of the Lisu, she had felt drawn to work among them. So she sent word to John that he must not ask for marriage until he had been told by the mission what part he was to work in. If God meant her to marry John, Isobel felt that He would send them to work in the same area. But before Isobel's letter reached China, John sent a letter to Vancouver. He had already been told where he was to work, and that was in

Yunnan Province, where the Lisu were! Would she marry him? She cabled back that she would.

Far away in China, John got the message. Travelling home on a bus in Shanghai afterwards, he felt so much in the clouds that he floated by the conductor and stepped off the bus without paying his fare! However the conductor was not so dreamy, and soon brought John's thoughts back to earth.

Back in Vancouver, it was not about bus travel Isobel was think-

ing. As the 11th of October drew near, she was thinking of her departure on the 'Empress of Russia' for China. When the big day came, a crowd gathered at the quay-side to say goodbye. Many young faces were there, and every one of them a proof that she had not been idle during her delay in Vancouver. She had been working in a Christian club for office girls, and some of those she had met had by now come to know the Lord.

As she looked across from the ship's deck to the quay, she could see tears on many faces. They were so sad to see her go. Isobel wanted so much to tell them again to follow Jesus, though she

[39]

was going away. She leaned over the rail, even as the ship was already pulling away from the quay, and across the water the girls heard a faint, slow voice quote the scripture verse: 'Let us go on'. Except for one, they did.

4 *Marriage motto*

ON the 4th of November, 1929, Isobel Miller married John Kuhn.

It was in Kunming that they were married (the capital of Yunnan) but their first home was in Chengchiang. It was a very small house, but that did not matter so much as the way it was made. It was right on the market street and it had no windows. Of course the front and back walls of the house could slide open, like those of the other houses, but this brought a problem – everyone could see in! Slowly Isobel realized: the Chinese did not care about living in privacy. In fact, if a house was closed off, people began to wonder just what was going on!

So she had to give up her privacy, but she was going to make the house as pretty as she could. She bought some good furniture, and a big rug covered the bumpy floor very nicely. The trunk she had brought from Vancouver was in the corner of the main room, and she covered it with a beautiful travelling rug.

When the first visitors arrived, Isobel knew that she must give them a warm welcome, for the Chinese themselves are noted for being kind to strangers. She seated her guests around the sitting room, and began to explain the gospel message as best she could.

How happy she was when she saw they understood, even though she had not long started to speak Chinese!

Then her heart sank. First of all an old lady, seated on the trunk, discovered that her nose was blocked. She promptly cleared her nose, wiping her fingers on Isobel's red and green travelling rug. Then a young mother lifted up her baby son and carried him to the door. But she was in no hurry, and a wet streak was left all the way along Isobel's other rug! She managed to keep her face bright, but inside she felt sick.

She kept talking till all her visitors chose to leave, and as she stood at the door called out the customary farewell: 'Travel slowly and come again'. Then she turned and went inside the house. So this was life as a missionary! She could not have pretty things. This was how life would be among the Chinese – they did not understand about pretty things. Her heart ached. She loved what was attractive, but she would have to forget about these things if she was to follow the Lord as she ought. Her eyes caught their marriage motto, hanging on the wall. It said, 'God first'. Now Isobel began to know what that was going to mean.

5 Kathryn Ann and Small Pearl

'BELLE, it's come! We are appointed to move west and take over the station of Tali!' Full of excitement, John waved the letter from headquarters in the air.

Isobel was delighted: Tali was one step nearer the Lisu tribes of which Mr Fraser had told her. Preparations were made, and at last they were on their way. Isobel was to make the long trek westwards more than once, but the first trip must have been quite special. Travel in those days was on foot, on horse-back, or by mountain chair. Whichever way you went the going was slow, and you had plenty of time to look around. The scenery was worth looking at: the mountains were high and the views from the top were breathtaking.

On the third day of the journey Isobel felt ill and had to rest for a time. So it was June 28th, 1930, before the last stage of the journey was reached. Poor Isobel was weak and tired, but at least the ground was level now. The mountains on the left rose to fifteen thousand feet, but on the right the rich green rice-fields sloped gently down to the edge of a large blue lake. On and on they went until Isobel said faintly:

'John, I can't go any farther'.

'Oh, you're doing fine, dear,' he encouraged her, 'just a few more steps. See, here is the gate.'

But she could not manage those steps. So John had to half carry her into her new home, and lay her on the floor. Then the Chinese pastor appeared, and did everything he could for their comfort. Pastor Li was a kind man, and the newcomers loved him from the start.

After a rest and some food, Isobel began to take a look at her new house. What a contrast to the windowless building back at Chengchiang! This house had three wings to it, with a front court and a back garden. Isobel could hardly believe that such space could be theirs. No wonder they called it 'the cloisters of Tali'!

But Tali was to be remembered for another reason, more than the spaciousness of their home. On the 10th of April, 1931, Kathryn Ann Kuhn was born. As soon as they could, the parents prayed over the tiny head of their first child: 'Lord, we give her back to Thee. We lay no claim to her. We want her to be Thine and serve Thee all her life.' Kathryn Ann was given a Chinese name as well as an English one. It was Hong-En (Vast Grace).

[When Hong-En grew up, she became a missionary herself, and went to tell the tribes of North Thailand about the great grace of God. Because of ill-health, however, she had to leave the work in 1968. She lives today with her husband in North America.]

The Kuhns had been at Tali for two-and-a-half years when they received the call to move west again. They had been quite happy working among the Chinese around Tali, but Isobel was always pleased to move nearer to her chosen Lisu.

★

The road to the west climbed up and up. It passed over the tops of lower mountains, only to begin to scale the heights of higher ones behind. It was wild, uninhabited country. They were nearing journey's end when the path, hung as it was in the clouds, suddenly fell away two thousand feet. Opposite where they were, they saw the next mountain range stand no higher than themselves. Looking down, they saw a little green patch far below. They felt they were on top of the world, but even from that distance they could see that a river ran through the valley below like a white silk thread. This was Yungping, the valley of Eternal Peace. At the end of it lay the little town of Old Market, where they were to live for the next two years.

It was here that the Kuhns really came to know Small Pearl. Her mother, Mrs Hwang, had been working for Isobel around the house at Tali. When they moved to Old Market, Isobel decided to take Mrs Hwang with her, and of course Small Pearl had to go too.

After a time, Mrs Hwang became a problem. She began to quarrel with everyone, and she was very lazy. When she went to shop at the market, she argued over prices so much that all the women there turned against her. Then one day she left. Some horsemen were passing through on their way to Tali, and she took the chance to go back with them.

What was Small Pearl to do? She had found her mother difficult too, and she liked staying with the Kuhns. Isobel offered to keep her as Kathryn's nursemaid, and Mrs Hwang agreed.

The work at Old Market proved difficult, but it was always a comfort to have Small Pearl. She was very good at caring for Kathryn, who needed all the attention she could get. She was a toddler and there was always a danger of her going too near the river which flowed in front of the house.

Although still only a young girl, Small Pearl came to believe in the Lord Jesus while at Old Nest. Her life-story as Mrs Yang is told in Isobel's exciting book, 'Nests Above the Abyss'.

6 Lisuland at last

DURING their time in Yungping, the Kuhns seemed to have little success. One or two ladies became interested in their message, as well as one young man named Ma Fu-Yin. They were discouraged at the time, but long after they were gone the seed they had sown here bore fruit in a harvest of souls.

When they had been at Yungping for some time, the Kuhns received another letter from Mr Fraser. He was asking them to visit the Lisu! They were to go for a month and see what they could do to help the church there. There was some trouble in the Lisu church, and the missionaries already there were finding it difficult to cope. Of course, Isobel was delighted to go.

Leaving little Kathryn behind with other missionaries, they began their long trek. First they went up the Mekong River valley, then they began to climb up the side of the valley to the mountain-top. What a view they had from there! They could even see the Lisu mountains in the far distance. They would love to have been able to jump right over, but first they had to come down. Into the Salween valley they descended, and when they had reached it the going got slow. There was no sign of human life, a noisy stream rushed past them, and they had to pick their way, climbing over rocks or walking carefully round them. They had been two hours in this jungle of rocks when the light began to fade and the rain began to fall. The village they were making for was called Old Nest, and they began to wonder if they would ever come to it. That morning, Isobel had been sick when they started out around six o'clock, but she managed to keep going till they reached Old Nest at last about seven in the evening.

They were again on the move with the first light of dawn, and by night time they stood at the door of Lisuland. After supper, John took Isobel out for a walk. It became dark, but the black mountain peaks stood out against the starry sky. Then there came light in the darkness – little moving specks of light up and down the mountains. They were fires, Lisu fires. Every fire meant a Lisu village, a village which was in heathen darkness, without the Light of the world. But the missionaries knew the Light of the world, and had come with news of Him to the Lisu. Oh, the thought of it filled Isobel's heart and thrilled it!

By the evening of the next day John and Isobel had reached Pine Mountain Village, where one of the two Lisu churches was. Isobel felt she was in a kind of paradise. As her eyes scanned the mountains, she picked out clumps of trees, outcrops of jagged rocks, and here and there a splash of colour from wild flowers. Even on rainy days Isobel could hardly take her eyes off the mountains: the mists then clothed them with a majesty which made her tremble.

Of course she had not come all the way from Vancouver to gaze at the mountains. There was work to do, and as Isobel lowered her eyes to survey the scene of future labours it was not pretty. The Lisu villages were filthy, and that brought nasty smells. Inside the homes the flies and other insects buzzed in thousands. The food was not too clean, and Isobel discovered that the people themselves just ate off a board on the mud floor. After a time, thought Isobel, they might learn to use a table.

But that was not the missionaries' first concern. What the people needed was food for their souls. They were starving, and the missionaries were glad to set before them in the word of God the Bread of Life.

*

The Kuhns did not stay long at Pine Mountain Village, but they stayed long enough to come to know Moses. The Moses of the Bible was so called because he was 'drawn out of the water'. This Lisu Moses might well have been so called because he was drawn out of heathendom. He was an attractive and clever man, but more than that, he was a sincere Christian. He had the gentle bearing of one who lives near to the Lord. However, when the Kuhns were with him, there was something tending to disturb Moses' peace of mind. His wife was expecting another child, and as none of her previous children had lived, it was expected that this one would be no exception. Then, ten days after the missionaries arrived, Moses' wife's baby arrived too. It was alive! Oh, what a thrill! Moses never left little Esther while she was awake. While she slept, he spent his time writing all his friends to say he now had a little girl.

Then one day a runner came to Pine Mountain Village. The message was from the other two white missionaries who were working among the Lisu in the north. It was for Moses, but it was delivered to the Kuhns. Isobel had to hand over the letter, though she could hardly bring herself to do it. It said –

'If Moses' baby has been born, please ask him to come up and help us here for three months. The work is spreading, so we need him.'

Isobel watched Moses' face as she delivered the message. For a moment he was startled – how could they ask him to leave his darling little child so soon, and for so long? Then he turned away and gazed across the canyon at the mountains on the opposite side. When he spoke again, his heart was at peace. He had looked to the Lord, and he said, 'I will go if the Lord wants me to go'. As Isobel watched him, she loved him for his selfless love to Christ, and in her heart she prayed: 'Lord, give us more Lisu like him'.

7 Partings

SOON the month in Lisuland was up: it was time to return. However, as the Lisu church still needed a missionary, it was decided that John should stay while Isobel went back without him.

To make the parting easier, John said he would go back with her part of the way. They left early in the morning, and climbed up and up, back and fore across the face of the Salween River Canyon. At one point the narrow path jutted out from the mountainside, and seemed to hang on nothing over the valley far below. However, about noon the path levelled off, and they found themselves on a broad plain. Here John decided to turn back, but first he called the carriers together for a parting prayer. Isobel liked such painful occasions to be over in a moment, but

John, being different, took his time over them. When he had finished his prayer, John began to sing:

'God be with you till we meet again . . . '

But when he was only half-way through the hymn, there was a shout, a sound of scampering animals, and all was confusion. Jasper, the mule which Isobel had been riding, had taken his chance to break away and John's horse had followed suit. As they looked down the trail up which they had just come, they saw the two animals disappearing with the Chinese attendant in vain pursuit! Now Isobel had no mule to ride on, and John had no horse to ride back. There was nothing for it but to trudge together down the trail they had just climbed up. It was late afternoon when they found Jasper – too late to start climbing again. So the parting which John had made so much of did not come that day!

★

After that first trip to Pine Mountain Village, John and Isobel were at last given permission to settle into their work among the Lisu. They moved in in December, 1934, but it was not very long before they were moving out again. There was a happy reason for their leaving, however – their furlough was overdue.

Isobel's mother had died years before this, but when the family got to Vancouver Grandpa Miller was there himself to meet them. They had told little Kathryn about the peppermints Grandpa always had, and she took to him at once. He was delighted, and from the first day they went everywhere together.

All good things come to an end, but the end to this first furlough was rather uncertain. First they were to sail, then they were not. They were booked to travel on a Japanese ship, but then war broke out between China and Japan, and the Mission Director told them at the last minute to wait. After getting the news, John and Isobel had their evening Bible reading and found themselves reading Psalm 91. They were so struck by the promises of divine protection that they asked permission to sail in spite of the danger. Their boat left the next day, so they slept little that night, waiting for a 'phone call at any moment. Then word came: they were to go! Everything had been packed, of course, so they only had to bundle themselves into a friend's car and make for the ship. That was on the last day of August, 1937.

★

Little Kathryn was six now: it was time for her to go to school. Her mother had thought about this, and intended putting her into a school in Yunnan. However, when the ship arrived at Hong-Kong, there was a telegram from headquarters. The way had opened for Kathryn to go to the big Mission school at Chefoo, and she was to go there from Hong Kong. Kathryn herself had been prepared for going to school by her mother's telling her she would have lots of other children to play with. But now it was the mother who was shocked, not the little girl. How could she part with her only child so suddenly?

If Isobel had known what was to happen to Kathryn at Chefoo, she would have felt the parting even more. The Japanese were to place the children in internment. But all this, of course, was hidden from an anxious mother at the time. In any case, the Lord cared for Kathryn when that time of trouble came. She was eventually taken back to America by ship, and was brought up there by Mission staff. When mother and daughter were reunited in the future, the years apart did not come between them at all. Thus the Lord fulfilled the promise which Isobel leaned on when she saw Kathryn's ship steam from Hong Kong in 1937: 'Cast thy bread upon the waters, for thou shalt find it after many days.' (Ecclesiastes 11 : 1)

8 'Behold, I am with thee'

AMID all changes, Isobel found her main encouragement and support to be the word of God. Two instances of this occurred at this stage of her life.

After waving goodbye to Kathryn at Hong Kong, the Kuhns returned to Yunnan. Here another shock awaited them. Mr Fraser had a meeting with them, and explained that he now wanted John Kuhn to become assistant superintendent for West Yunnan. This would mean that the Kuhns would not return to Lisuland, as they had expected.

Isobel was shattered. So long before, she had felt the Lord's call to live among the Lisu: now it was not going to be. She went aside to pray with a broken heart. Then suddenly the Lord spoke to her through His word: 'I will bring you again' (Zephaniah 3:20). She spoke to no-one about it – not even to John – but she felt sure that the Lord would bring her back to Lisuland again.

Of course for the present they went to Paoshan, as Mr Fraser had directed. They had been there scarcely two months, however, when Mr Fraser got in touch again. The Lisu church was in difficulty, and needed guidance. John and Isobel were to go for a short visit, and then return to Paoshan. At once Isobel felt that this was the word of God fulfilled to her. Mr Fraser had told them to return for a little while, but Isobel felt she was now facing the main stage in her life's work. She was quite right. They were about to return to Paoshan when Mr Fraser died, and all missionaries stayed where they were for the time being. At other times also it was planned that the Kuhns leave Lisuland, but it never came about.

★

Another special case of the Lord fulfilling His word to Isobel came in 1942.

In March of that year she began to suffer from toothache. The nearest dentist was at the other end of the Province, but she knew she would have to see him. When she reached Paoshan she heard of two American airmen who were leaving the next day by car for Kunming – her own destination. She was glad of the lift, though she had to be ready by five-thirty a.m. to get it. She woke at four o'clock, and wondered sleepily whether to have her normal Bible-reading, or whether to sleep for another half-hour. She decided to get up, and when she opened her Bible she found herself reading the old story of Jacob's dream. That morning, one verse stood out as never before: 'And behold I am with thee, and will keep thee in all places whither thou goest, and will bring thee again into this land' (Genesis 28 : 15). She did not know it then, but she was to need that verse many times before she saw Paoshan again.

By the time Isobel got east to Kunming and had her tooth extracted, things had changed drastically. The Japanese had come in from the west and had bombed Paoshan. Everywhere was chaos and confusion. Rumours of the war reached Kunming, and refugees began to flee the area. What must Isobel do? She asked the Lord for guidance, but did not receive any. Everyone was telling her to flee, and in the end she did. An RAF convoy was travelling north from Kunming and she was given a place in the back of a truck. For six days she stayed with the convoy as it pressed on northwards. All along the bumpy road she was tortured with doubt. Had she done wrong in fleeing from Kunming without the Lord's direction? Then she remembered the promise to Jacob, as he too had been fleeing: 'And behold I am with thee, and will keep thee in all places whither thou goest, and will bring thee again into this land.' Her sleepy eyes had read these words back in Paoshan: now she was wide awake to their meaning. It was some time before the promise was fulfilled, and in the interval she had many trials. In the end, however, God brought her in a wonderful way, not only to Paoshan, but to Oak Flat itself.

9 Bible School

OAK FLAT is the name of the village where the Kuhns had settled, when they eventually moved into their work among the Lisu. Their shanty here was a little apart from the rest of the village, set on the edge of a sheer drop in the mountain slope. This gave them a beautiful view: it also gave them some privacy.

During the winter months the missionaries travelled around the Lisu villages, holding Bible studies where they were invited. The Lisu people, of course, lived off the land, so they had to spend most of the year caring for their crops. During the rainy season, however, it was possible for them to leave their homes, and Isobel had the idea of holding Bible classes at Oak Flat during these months.

A Bible School for girls was planned for February, 1943, but when the time drew near no girls would promise to come. The Japanese were around, and the girls were afraid that if they left home they might not get back again because of the war. There was a lot of work in preparing for the Bible School, but the missionaries decided to go on with it, even without the promise of one student.

The School was due to start on a Monday, and by Saturday a dozen girls turned up. They were all from the same side of the Salween River as Oak Flat. But Isobel specially wanted the girls from the west bank to attend as they somehow were better students.

As well as the war situation, there was another reason why the girls from the west bank might not come. A winter storm had broken out, and these sometimes lasted for two weeks. An icy wind was blowing, and heavy rain never ceased to fall. How could the girls be expected to walk twenty miles and cross the Salween River in a storm? But still Isobel hoped and prayed and went on preparing.

Monday brought a sudden lull in the storm, though the clouds

still hung in heavy wreaths around the mountain tops. The Bible School began as planned in the morning, but Isobel's eyes must often have glanced longingly up the trail, searching for her best pupils. Hope had almost died, but at sunset a shout rang out: 'Girls from the west bank are coming!' Teacher and pupils ran to the door and looked up. There they were – a thin line of dots breaking away from the low cloud and winding down the Oak Flat trail. A little longer and Isobel could make them out – yes, there were Mary, Lydia, Julia, Chloe and others, their bedding and books carried in big bags on their backs.

'We were afraid you wouldn't make it', shouted Isobel. But the looks on the girls' faces showed they wouldn't have missed coming for all the world. They had hardly settled in when the storm broke again, and continued for a week.

In August of that year Isobel's second child was born. She had a boy this time and she called him Danny. Daddy was delighted; the Chinese always look on a son as a greater honour than a daughter. For twelve years he had had only a daughter. Now he could hold his head high when asked the frequent question: 'What children do you have?'

The Bible School for 1944 brought the greatest worries of all. Charles Peterson (the other missionary at Oak Flat) was away on sick leave when February came round. John was to be at home, but he came down with 'flu! Poor Isobel had to struggle on, teaching the girls on her own, but she somehow managed.

March was the month for the Boys' Bible School. These were mainly of the 12 - 14 age group: most of them were cowherds, but they were able at this time of year to get older boys to do their work for them. Now Isobel really had problems! John, now recovered from the 'flu, had to go off to a Mission Conference. Charles Peterson was still on sick leave. And the School was completely out of pencils, jotters, paper and ink. What was Isobel to do? She was tempted to panic, but she refused. Instead, she prayed in faith. She had asked the Lisu church for two evangelists to help her run the school. One had turned up, but the other had been refused a military pass, so she prayed that the way would open for him to come.

The Lord answered these prayers above what Isobel had asked or thought. First, evangelist Thomas arrived from the west side, bringing some pupils with him. The next morning, in came the longed-for pencils, paper, etc., all the way from Paoshan. Thirdly, out of the blue, in dropped Charlie Peterson. So, what had looked like being a failure turned into the biggest success of all!

[54]

10 'A covert from the tempest'

IN October, 1944, the Kuhns went home for their second furlough. It was a long one, partly because of the war. John himself returned to China in January 1946, but Isobel and Danny did not follow till the next year.

When at last she saw Oak Flat again, Isobel found many changes. First she noticed their house. It had an unhealthy slant towards the edge of the precipice in front of it, and most of the thatched roof had been blown off. Inside, the furniture was all covered with dust.

Gradually, she began to notice other changes as well. Many in the church were constant, but she did not like the spirit of Keh-de-seh-pa. He had power in Oak Flat Village, and as deacon in the church he wanted power there too. When the post of local teacher fell vacant, he demanded the position for his second son. The other Lisu were afraid of him, but Isobel said 'No!' Then things began to happen. Goats from the Mission herd were lost, and the water supply was cut off.

In the mercy of God, John was at home when matters came to a head. The worldly section of the village marched up to the church one Sabbath evening, and there would have been a fight if John had not intervened. When he came home, John buried his face in his hands. It looked like defeat – defeat after thirteen years. It certainly meant one thing: Isobel could not live any longer alone in Oak Flat. Across the Salween River Canyon there was another village, called Village of Olives. It was decided that Isobel must move there as quickly as possible.

It was December 1948 when Isobel moved. Early in 1949, a band of brigands invaded Oak Flat, their leader asking where

Isobel was. In the past, she had upset the plots of this wicked man and he had come to seek revenge. What a blessing that she was not there! Nor was this the only reason why God in His providence had shifted the Mission centre to the other side of the river gorge. There was a heathen tribe there which had never been reached with the gospel. The time would soon be when white missionaries would have to leave China altogether, but God saw that this tribe was reached before that time.

This was the wonderful thing about these days of fear and turmoil. God saw that His work went on as before. The 1948 Bible School had carried on as usual, held as it was amid war and rumours of war. A group of students had even come all the way from Burma; one of them had been walking for seventeen days! The same happened in 1949. The Bible School was in full swing when news came that a group of brigands was approaching Oak Flat. They had already taken Luchang, to the south of Village of Olives, and they were expected to march north immediately. Isobel and Charles Peterson expected the hundred or so students to flee at once to the safety of their mountain homes, but they all stayed on. This was in May, the driest and hottest month.

Then suddenly it began to rain. Day after day it poured down, till the mountain streams turned into raging torrents. The rains had come a full month early, but they had come to stay. This meant that the invaders were pinned down at Luchang. Village of Olives was only a morning's march to the north, but it was a morning's march too far. They could not move a step. Instead they sat and fretted at the rain, while the missionaries and the Christian Lisu praised God for the peace He had given them to study His word.

★

As 1949 drew to a close, Isobel began to think a lot about Danny. He was past his sixth birthday now, and should be going to school.

She was hardly seeing John now; he was so much on trek, visiting churches here and there. She made up her mind the only thing was to take Danny home to America and put him to school there. It was dangerous letting him grow up among tribal children, for he could not but learn their heathen ways.

Then Isobel remembered 1942. That was the year in which she had fled from Kunming, and had found afterwards that it had not been really necessary. She hesitated. 1950 dawned, and in walked John. The Lord seemed always to send him home when he was most needed! They discussed together the problems of staying on – the danger of Danny's young mind being harmed and the daily threat of invasion. John agreed with Isobel – she must take Danny home.

But before that – what about one last Bible School? It was not the proper season, but they thought the Lisu would not mind. They were right. Awkward as it may have been, one hundred students came to the thirteenth and last season of Bible study to be held in the Salween Canyon. As before, there was another river in that Canyon besides the Salween. The river of the water of life flowed there, and how gladly believing sinners drank from its streams!

11 Long trek

IT was time now to leave: Isobel knew that to delay longer might mean that she and Danny would never get out. The Communists were all around them, and would very soon take charge of Village of Olives. The parting with Daddy came on 10th March: it was the hardest parting of all. John was usually so bright, but this time as he watched Isobel's party move away, his face could not hide the sadness of his heart.

West of Village of Olives was a high mountain range; on the other side of these mountains lay Burma. So to get to Burma Isobel and Danny had to get over the Pien Ma Pass which stood 10,998 feet high. On the evening of the third day's climb they slept in the last house before the Pass. They thought they were well on their way, but next morning came disappointment with the patter of rain on the roof. The carriers were disheartened: they knew that the rain would fall as snow higher up on the Pass, and spoke of returning to Village of Olives. They were Christian Lisu, and were not without courage: they simply felt it was senseless to go on. Isobel prayed, and then made a proposal. If it was not raining the next morning, they would take it as a sign they should press on. If it was raining, they would turn back.

Early next morning Isobel woke and crossed to the door to look out. The clouds were heavy and low, but there was no rain. She called the others. They dressed and ate hurriedly, and left. As they did so they heard loud protests from their host: he was saying that they would never make it! They knew it would take the whole long morning to reach the top, so they hurried on their way. Once a blink of cheering sunlight shone on them, but then the sun disappeared and the rain drizzled down. By the time the rain had stopped the party was actually climbing through the clouds, so they hardly knew where they were. Isobel was worried: should she endanger the lives of these men with her – should they not all return to safety? She was praying for guidance when two figures loomed up in the mist ahead. They were the first of a party of Lisu who had just crossed the pass from the Burma side! Struggling on with new hope, Isobel soon met another two from the same party. One of them said: 'It's beginning to snow on the top of the pass, but you can make it. Watch for our footprints;

there is nothing else to show where the trail is.' It was now mid-day, and they had eaten nothing since very early. But they dared not waste a moment; they knew they had to press on. The trail over the pass itself was no broader than a cowpath, and it was just as they came to it that they met the last of the other party. Their feet had so recently sunk into the snow that the path was still quite clear. Marvelling at the mercy of God, Isobel and her carriers hurried over the pass: they knew they had just seen a miracle of God's providence.

Coming down the western side, the path got more and more slippery. In the end, Isobel had to dismount and walk. The snow had been melting and running as icy water into her wellingtons, so that her legs had no feeling below the knees. Somehow, however, they carried her over those last slippery miles to shelter.

Of course, the journey home had only now begun. It had begun with toil and strain, but it had also begun with God's care and blessing. And so it went on, through Burmese jungles to Rangoon, from Rangoon to Hong Kong, from Hong Kong to Vancouver. All the way Isobel felt her need, but all the time she got that strength which is made perfect in weakness.

12 Last climb

IT was pleasant for Isobel and Danny to be together with Kathryn again, who had now almost completed her studies. But they could not forget Lisuland, for Daddy was still there.

He was not there for long, however. The Mission decided to

take all workers out of China, as their presence now endangered the native Church. China was now under the Communists. Did this mean the end of the China Inland Mission? No – the work was to go on, though in a different part. From now on the Mission would work among Chinese who lived outside China, and among other heathen peoples.

Soon the Mission became interested in starting work in Thailand. Before John went home, they asked him to see how things were in that country. Hearing of this at home, Isobel began to worry: would John offer himself for work in Thailand without telling her? She wrote to ask him not to do so.

As John toiled over the mountains of North Thailand in the summer of 1951, Isobel sat at home and read a book by one of her favourite writers – Amy Carmichael. But suddenly something in the book disturbed her comfort: it was a passage entitled, 'Climb or die'. Miss Carmichael was saying that the servant of Jesus Christ must follow his Lord fully, not resting to the end of his days in this world. Isobel's mind went back to the Pien Ma Pass which she and Danny had crossed the year before. Then it had been a case of 'climb or die': if they had rested on the lower slopes of the snowy mountain they would have died there. She felt it like that now in her life of following the Lord Jesus. There was work to be done in Thailand and she must do it: there were peaks to be climbed there and she must climb them. Certainly there were missionaries going out to work there who were young and strong, but Isobel knew that they needed the kind of guidance which John and she could give. So it was decided: she would climb on. The story of Isobel's 'Ascent to the Tribes' of Thailand is told in her own charming book of that name. Some time you must read it for yourselves.

*

It was during the summer of 1952 that Isobel and John returned to the work. In November, 1954, Isobel was flown home, dying of cancer. As she saw her own lifework draw to a close, she saw her daughter Kathryn's just begin. Accepted now as a missionary, she was to sail in February, but *must* she sail so soon? In the end she did, for Isobel knew it would be wrong to keep her.

During these months Isobel was quite weak. She made good use of what strength she had, however, as the books she now wrote clearly testify. Then in the summer of 1955 John came home! It was a wonderful reunion, though they met under the shadow of a parting soon to come.

At the beginning of the next year Isobel sent a letter to her older brother. Here is a little of what she wrote, as she looked back on her life.

'You say I have a life well-lived. I am glad that I gave my life to Christ when I was young, but that is not my satisfaction. I am trusting only in Christ's merits for salvation; my own life has been too full of faults and failures to be worth anything . . .

'I don't know how people face life with its trials without Him: I know many just try not to think. That is so sad to me . . . I am so grateful He led me to Himself when I was young so that I could have this long earthly walk with Him. I recommend Him as a peerless Master'.

That peerless Master came to her bedside on the 10th of March, 1957, and took her to Himself. John was the only one present at that glorious hour. Afterwards he said, 'If ever I was near heaven, and if ever I was conscious that death has lost its sting, it was then.'

BILLY BRAY

1 *Billy is born, then born again*

PROBABLY there were not so many as twelve houses in Twelve-heads. But Twelveheads, tiny Cornish village that it was, had a chapel of its own. Billy's grandfather had helped to build it, long before Billy was born on June 1st, 1794.

Billy's grandfather saw a lot of him and his brothers and sisters – they lived just down the road. He saw even more of them when Billy's father died. The children moved along the village to their grandfather's home, and there they were brought up.

★

When Billy was seventeen, he left Twelveheads and moved to Devon. Here he married, and here he stayed till he was twenty-four. He lived a wild life in Devon. By the time he saw Cornwall again he was a thorough drunkard, making his poor wife miserable.

One day Billy took a barrow and went off for coal. His wife watched for him, and waited and waited. At last she left the house to look for him. She saw a barrow of coal outside a beer-shop and she knew it was his. She had to take the coal home herself, while Billy spent his money getting drunk.

★

But all this time, Billy was afraid. He knew that he was living a sinful life and he knew that sinners are on the way to hell. He came across a book by John Bunyan – 'Visions of Heaven and Hell'. He read it, and as he read his fears grew even greater.

He knew he should pray for mercy, but he was afraid to go on his knees. If his wife saw him, she might despise him as a coward. He hoped his wife would be converted first, then it would be easy for him to begin to pray.

Then one night, a thought occurred to Billy. Perhaps it would be too late for him, if he waited till his wife was converted. It was three o'clock in the morning, but Billy jumped straight out of bed and went on his knees.

He had not prayed before, but now that he had started he would not stop. He felt very downcast, and he was afraid God could not show mercy to such a great sinner as he. What a burden he carried, at home and at work! He cried under the load, until one of his work-mates told him to make less noise. But Billy replied, 'You would roar out too, if you felt my load; and roar I will until I get it off'.

Although he had not yet received forgiveness for his sins, Billy had left off his sinful habits and was seeking the Lord. It was an encouragement to him to know that he was seeking the Lord, for he felt, 'I would rather be crying for mercy than living in sin'.

Every day and every night he prayed. Then, at his work one day, the thought came to him that he might never find mercy. This thought was from the devil, and Billy knew it. 'Thou art a liar, devil', said Billy, and this encouraged him to go on praying for mercy. He had resisted the devil, and that night he sought the Lord with fresh desire.

When he got home, he went to his bedroom and closed the door: 'I said to the Lord, "Thou hast said, They that ask shall receive, they that seek shall find, and to them that knock, the door shall be opened, *and I have faith to believe it*".'

His wife heard a noise: it was Billy shouting. It was not a drunken song she heard, nor was it now the anguished cry for mercy. It was a new song, coming from a new man. It was the shout of deliverance – a song of joy in the Lord, such as David had long ago:

'He brought me up out of an horrible pit, out of the miry clay, and set my feet upon a rock, and established my goings. And he hath put a new song in my mouth, even praise unto our God.' (Psalm 40 : 3-4).

Billy had passed through a great change. As the Bible puts it, he had been 'born again'.

2 *The new Billy Bray*

HAPPINESS now became a marked feature of Billy's life. His happiness was real, and he did not try to conceal it. Some did not like him shouting and singing for joy. But Billy would reply:

'You must know that the Devil is not deaf either, and yet his servants make a great noise. The Devil would rather see us doubting than hear us shouting . . . If they were to put me in a barrel, I would shout "glory" out through the bunghole. I can *say* glory, glory: I can *sing* glory, glory: I can *dance* glory, glory.'

This happiness Billy had, even as he walked along the street: 'I lift up one foot, and it seems to say "glory", and I lift up the other, and it seems to say, "Amen": and so they keep on like that all the time that I am walking.'

★

Another feature of Billy's life after his conversion was his love to others who were lost as he had been. Everyone he met he told how happy he now was. He told them, because he wanted them to seek happiness in the same way.

Billy used to work in a tin mine, and the work was dangerous. When he was converted, he began to pray with the other men at the mine, before they went down the shaft. Time and time again, these hard miners would hear Billy pray:

'Lord, if any of us must be killed, or die, today, let it be me. Let not one of these men die, for they are not happy. But I am, and if I die today, I shall go to heaven.'

Many of them wept to hear Billy pray in such a loving way, and some became praying men themselves.

But a man cannot be judged merely by his feelings or his words. He must be judged by what he *does*.

Near Billy's home there lived an old man and his son. They lived just as Billy had done before his conversion. Billy began to visit them, and to tell them that the Lord was willing to save them too. Then he would pray with them, and sometimes the old man would have tears in his eyes when Billy got off his knees. But as Billy walked away he would hear the old man swearing at his son, and sometimes he was tempted not to visit the house again. But he continued to speak to them and pray with them, and, before he died, the old man 'was made very happy in Jesus'.

Someone else who was converted through Billy's witness had been his companion when he was a drunkard. When Billy would warn his mates about the danger of sin, they used to make fun of him. But Billy's former friend would check the men for this. Instead of mocking Billy, he used to say, 'I wish I was like him'. Billy then felt drawn to this man, and he began to pray for him. One day when Billy was working in a field he felt he should pray for him, so he knelt down where he was and prayed. In the middle of the prayer, Billy felt the Lord was saying to him, 'I will save him soon'. And so He did.

Soon afterwards, this man became ill. Billy often went to see him and took back this report: 'He told me he was happy in Jesus, and going to heaven to praise God for ever'.

Another man who could bless God that he met Billy Bray was a work-mate of his. For a time they were separated, then one Monday evening it came into Billy's mind that, if he went to see this man, he would be saved. He did go, and the man was saved, after Billy had spoken to him and prayed with him.

Afterwards this man, too, became ill. As he lay on his bed dying, he sent for Billy Bray. When he saw Billy, he gave a great shout, 'Christ is mine, and I am His'. Then he lay back and died in peace.

This, then, was the effect conversion had on Billy – it made him happy, and it made him loving. Billy knew that some despised him, as one who showed too openly his happiness and his love. But he was unconcerned:

'They said I was a mad-man, but they meant I was a glad-man. And glory be to God, I have been glad ever since.'

3 Chapel-building

A LITTLE while after Billy was converted, you could have seen a crowd of people gathered in the open air at Cross Lanes. (Cross Lanes was a little village near to Twelveheads.) If you had got near the front of the crowd, you would have seen a minister standing on a stone, preaching. When he finished, a wiry little man stood up on the stone, and began to address the crowd. He looked over them with quick, sharp eyes, and said:

'If this new chapel, which they say is to be called Bethel, stands one hundred years, and one soul be converted in it every year, that will be one hundred souls, and one soul is worth more than all Cornwall.' The little man then danced on the stone, which was the foundation stone of a new chapel, and shouted, 'Glory, glory, bless the Lord'. Yes, it was little Billy Bray.

The idea of building a chapel at Cross Lanes had been Billy's own. His mother had given him a piece of ground there, and he had cleared away the hedge and dug the foundation himself.

For the work of building up the walls, Billy had to employ masons. He had no money to pay them, but the Lord took care of that. Then Billy met with a difficulty – he had not quite enough wood for the roof. He was short of a principal, which is a strong beam used to support the end of a roof. Billy asked his 'heavenly Father to send some timber, or money to buy some'.

In a little while a Christian man, moved by God, came down to where Billy was working at the chapel, and asked, 'What do you want a pound note for?' Billy replied, 'To buy timber to put a principal up on *that* end of the chapel'.

The chapel was nearly finished, but still there was wood needed for the door and windows and seats. A mine had recently been closed, and Billy was given money to buy some of the timber that was being sold off.

But it was one thing to buy timber at the mine – it was another thing to have the timber at the chapel, where it was needed. Billy asked a neighbour for the loan of a horse and cart. The neighbour said the horse would never pull a cart, but Billy still asked for the loan of it. How did he get on?

'I never saw a better horse in all my life; I did not touch her with whip or stick, though we had steep hills to come up over. When I took back the mare, and told my neighbour, "I never saw a better mare", he said, "I never saw such a thing; she will not draw with any one else".' The owner of the mare was surprised, but Billy was not, and he had his explanation:

'That mare was working that day for a very strong company – Father, Son and Holy Ghost, whom horses, angels, men and devils must obey. If there had been no one there more powerful than Billy Bray, she would have been as bad with him as with anybody else. But, bless and praise the name of the dear Lord, He said, "The horse shall work, for the timber is to seat my house" – and what the dear Lord says shall be obeyed.'

★

Kerley Downs was about a mile from Billy's home. When Billy had completed the new chapel at Cross Lanes, the Lord directed him to build one at Kerley Downs as well. A farmer offered a piece of land as a site, and gave Billy the loan of a horse and cart for carrying stones to the site. Some of the congregation promised to help Billy, but he soon found that their promises were not sincere. He was left to do all the work himself.

Billy seemed to be everywhere those days. He might work in the morning at the mines, and be at the chapel for the afternoon and evening. Or he might spend the morning building, and be at the mine for the rest of the day. Sometimes he worked altogether twenty hours in a day. And on the Lord's Day, he was not idle. Sometimes he had to walk twenty miles, and preach three times.

The chapel was almost finished now, and Billy wondered where he would get a pulpit. He went to an auction sale, where he spied an old three-cornered cupboard. 'The very thing', he thought. 'I'll soon knock that into a pulpit.'

Billy didn't know much about auction sales. He asked a man nearby how much the cupboard would sell for. 'Six shillings', he was told. What was more, this man handed Billy the six shillings with which to buy the cupboard. Billy was delighted, and waited impatiently for the cupboard to go up for sale.

When it was put up for auction, the people in the room heard a loud voice shout, 'Here's six shillings for it: I want it for a pulpit.' The people at the sale began to laugh a little – why, Billy didn't know.

'Six shillings, going for six', shouted the auctioneer.

'Seven', said a voice from behind Billy. Next moment, the cupboard was sold, and not to him. Puzzled and downhearted, Billy turned to return the six shillings to the man beside him. But he had gone. What was Billy to do now with the man's money?

He did what he always did in trouble. He went and prayed about it in the little chapel. Not much later, he appeared again, quite confident that all would end well.

Then he saw something being carted up the hill. It couldn't be – yes it was – the cupboard he had missed at the sale! Billy decided to follow the cupboard, to see where it finished up. Along the road, the cart stopped at a house. The cupboard was unloaded, and the men took it to the door of the house. But it wouldn't go in. They tried it this way and that, but after a great struggle the cupboard was still outside the house. The owner was angry. To think of it! He had paid seven shillings for it, and he would only get firewood out of it now!

Then Billy stepped forward with the six shillings in his hand. 'I'll give you six shillings for it', he said, 'if you'll carry it down to the chapel'. The man was delighted; now he would lose only one shilling instead of seven.

'Bless the Lord', said Billy, ' 'tis just like Him. He knew I couldn't carry it myself, so He got this man to carry it for me.'

The third chapel which Billy built was at Gwennap, a good distance from his home. He worked at the mine by night, and quarried stones for building by day. He chose a spot by the railway to dig for stones. Others had been digging there before him, but they had worked only at two sides, judging the area in the middle to be worthless. People were amazed at the stones that Billy dug out of that patch in the middle. But Billy was not amazed: he just remarked, 'The dear Lord helped me, as He said'.

So Billy gathered a great pile of stones on the site. Then he employed masons to build the chapel walls. How did he pay the masons? There are a few stories about how the Lord provided for this.

While collecting support in Helston, Billy found himself

standing at the door of a miser's house. He knew the miser never gave any money to support anything, but still he knocked at the door. The man came out, but told Billy he could not afford to part with any money.

Then Billy did some straight talking. 'You *can* give me some money, and if you do not you may soon die, and leave it all behind.'

The miser replied, 'Go round the town and see what you can get, and come to me again by-and-by.'

But Billy could not be put off. 'No, you have got money, and I must have some now.' The man put his hand in his pocket, but it stayed there. Then Billy told him what the Lord would do with greedy people. The man's hand went in and out of his pocket. Billy knew he had plenty of money, but it was clear that there would be a struggle before he got any of it for the Lord's house. For a time, the man talked. Was he going to talk all day? At last his hand came right out of his pocket and he handed Billy two shillings and sixpence. Some people said afterwards it was the greatest miracle ever performed in Helston.

Among other places, Billy went to St Ives. He was told he had come at a poor time. The fishing people had hardly enough to eat, as they were catching no fish.

But Billy knew what to do about that. He went to a prayer meeting, and asked the Lord to send some fish. After this meeting, they went a while to a coffee-house. They then began another prayer meeting, specially to pray for fish. They prayed till midnight.

As they made their way home in the moonlight, they met some women who were very poor. They were smiling, however, for they carried plates stacked with pilchards. Many a home got a welcome store of food that night. By next day, eight thousand casks of fish were landed.

But what had the fishing at St Ives to do with a new chapel at Gwennap? One of the fishermen told Billy to get a boat and come out to sea. A carpenter provided a boat, and to sea they went. The fishermen caught the fish, and threw them into Billy's boat. When they got back to the land, the carpenter sold Billy's fish for him, and brought in £6 15s. for the chapel. Altogether, Billy left St Ives with £17. When he got home he found he had enough to pay the masons and carpenters to finish the chapel completely.

4 *Billy's faith*

BILLY'S wife was one day lying sick in bed. She was a Christian, but at this time down-hearted. She complained to Billy: 'William, I do not *see* anything from heaven'.

'Neither do I, and what need has the Lord to show us sights when we can believe without it? If I saw the Saviour a babe in the manger, I should not believe it more than I do now. If I saw him raise Lazarus out of the grave, I should not believe it more than I do now. If I saw the Lord Jesus raise the ruler's daughter or the widow's son to life, I should not believe it more than I do now. And if I saw the dear Lord nailed to the cross, and heard Him cry, "It is finished", saw Him give up the ghost, and rise from the tomb the third day, I should not believe these things more than I do now.'

The above is a *statement* of Billy's faith. Here now are some proofs of it.

One day, sickness again visited Billy's home. This time, it was one of Billy's children who lay ill. Billy's wife asked him to go to the doctor for some medicine.

This was not so easily done then as it is today. Medicines had to be paid for in those days. But Billy, poor as he was, put eighteen pence in his pocket and set off for the doctor's house.

Along the road, he met a man begging. This man told Billy he had lost his cow, and needed money to buy another. Billy believed the man was really in need, and gave him all the money that was in his pocket.

Of course, it was of no use now to go for the doctor. But

there was a hedge nearby, and a place to pray. So Billy jumped the hedge, and 'told Father all about it'.

Some people might have wondered what Billy was doing, jumping hedges back and fore, but Billy didn't mind. When he got on to the road again, and started back home, he was full of faith that his little child would live. When he got home he said, 'Joey, the child's better, isn't it?'

'Yes', she said. 'The child will live'; said Billy calmly, 'the Lord has told me so.'

One morning Billy appeared in the door of his house with a child in each arm. Joey said:

'Billy, where are you going with the children?'

'The mother's dead, and the father's run away and left them, and I thought I'd bring them in, and rear them up with ours.'

'But we have four of our own that you can only just maintain, and these must go to the workhouse.'

But Billy's mind was made up. He believed that the Lord could give them means to support the children, and he would not turn them out. So he set the little boy and girl down among his own children, saying, 'Here, my dears, this is your home now'.

At that moment, there was another stranger in the home. He was a Christian too, and better off than Billy was. He saw what took place between Billy and his wife, and thought to himself, 'I am quite well off, and have no children to support. Yet I would be afraid to take two strange children into my home'. This visitor had £2 15s. 10d. in his pocket. He gave five shillings to Billy towards maintaining the children. Billy immediately shouted,

'There, Joey, the Lord has sent five shillings already, although the children have not eaten a penny loaf.'

Seeing how much five shillings had meant to Billy, the stranger gave five shillings more.

'Praise the Lord! Joey, didn't I tell you the Lord could feed them here?'

[76]

After a minute the man doubled his gift to Billy, giving him another ten shillings.

'Hallelujah! for the Lord will provide', was the response.

After this, the visitor took up a book and began to read. But his mind was not on his book; it was on the other £1 15s. 10d. still in his pocket. 'Lord, what am I to do?' was his anguished cry. 'Give Billy more', was the clear reply.

'Billy, I have not given you enough yet; take another sovereign.'

'Glory be to God! Cheer up, Joey, the money is coming!'

Again the visitor tried to settle, but found he could not. Not while he still had 15s. 10d. in his pocket. He gave ten shillings, and finally he gave over the last 5s. 10d. But Billy refused the ten pence.

'No brother, keep that to pay turnpike-gates when you go home.' (Billy referred to dues which travellers had to pay on the roads in those days.)

Billy's faith regarding the Lord's care over these little children was now rewarded, and he wanted to praise. 'Let's have a little prayer', he suggested. And pray he did, and while he prayed the visitor thought, 'I have never felt such divine power; I never expect such a blessing again, this side of heaven.'

★

Billy's faith took in every aspect of his life; it included his work, as well as his home and family.

At one time, Billy had a job at the mine which involved emptying a shaft when it filled with water. The shaft filled up every twelve hours. On one occasion, it came to his turn to empty the shaft on the Lord's Day. But before Billy left the church to go to the mine, a thought occurred to him. It was the Lord's Day, and it was not necessary for the shaft to be emptied then, so he would leave it till Monday.

Early Monday morning, Billy arrived at the mine to do his job. But the 'Captain' at the mine was waiting for him.

'Why were you not here yesterday?'

'It is the Lord's will that I should not work on Sundays.'

'I'll Lord's will thee. Thou shalt not work here any more.'
Billy's faith did not forsake him in the face of this outburst. 'For
I felt', he said, 'that I had the Lord of rocks and hills for my
Friend, and I did not care who was against me.'

After a time, the 'Captain' relented, and gave Billy a job at
which he did not need to work on the Lord's Day. About the
same time, Twelveheads Chapel became the scene of a revival, and
many souls were converted. Billy felt now that he should leave
his new work altogether for a time, as he was needed in the chapel
every day. He thought twice about staying off on Friday, though.
Friday was the day men were taken on for the work of the
following week. But in the end he stayed in the chapel at the
Lord's work.

That night two men came to the Chapel. They called for Billy.
When he came out they told him that he had been appointed to
work with them at the mine. Billy's faith had once more been
rewarded:

'So I stayed that week and worked for the Lord; and on Monday morning I went to see the place that the Lord had got for me.
At the place I had been turned away from I got only £2 a month;
and in this new place I had £5 a month or more, and had not to
work so hard by a great deal. And so the Lord cleared my way
for ever from working Sundays. I did not lose by serving the
Lord, but got £3 a month more than I got before; and did the
will of the Lord, which is better than all the money in the world.'

★

Even in the matter of clothing, Billy believed that his heavenly
Father would provide for him.

Coming home from preaching one evening, Billy found himself trudging along a road which had become very sticky with

mud. Each step he took, it was getting harder to pull his foot out of the soft earth. Then it happened. His foot came smartly up as he struggled to lift it – but the sole of his shoe had been left behind! He now had only half a shoe on his foot. He took the

half off. Holding it up heaven-ward, he said, 'Here, Father, thou knowest that I have worn out these shoes in Thy cause, and I have no money to buy new ones. Help me.'

The next week a friend of Billy's called and asked him to go to Truro. When they got there, the preacher was taken first to a shoe shop, where he was fitted with a new pair of shoes. Then he was taken to some other shops in Truro, and given other necessary clothing as well. The prayer Billy had offered as he stood in the mud had now been answered more abundantly than he had asked or thought.

5 *Attacked by Satan*

EVERY believer in the Lord Jesus is tried some way or other by Satan. Billy knew this for himself. As he used to say – 'The Devil knows where I live'.

Sometimes Satan would suggest to Billy to throw himself down the mineshaft. But Billy would reply that the Devil should do it himself, and see how he liked it.

Once Satan attacked Billy just as he was completing one of the chapels. His children were young at the time, and he was concerned about one of them, for she was very ill.

The Devil said: 'The church roof will cost £7; you have only £2. Your daughter will die, it will cost £1 to bury her, and that will leave you with £1 to finish the church.'

Billy's thoughts ran to and fro from his sick child to his unfinished chapel. Then a thought came to him. The Lord would reward him for working at the church by healing his child. He went home quite happily and told Joey their child would live.

Joey was doubtful. All the neighbours said the child would die and at that moment it looked as if *they* would be right, and not Billy. That night, the child grew worse, and the next day she was no better.

At lunch-time Billy came home. The little girl lay near the window of the room as her father prayed:

'Dear Lord, thou hast said that my child shall live, but she has not eaten any bread yet.' There and then, the child began to eat. She lived to be the mother of ten children.

Billy said afterwards: 'So the Lord made the Devil a liar once more. The Devil did not do me any hurt; he only made me bolder.'

★

When Billy was an old man, he was one day in his potato patch pulling up shaws (the stems of potatoes). He lifted one shaw, and the next, and the next, but no potatoes came up. The crop had failed that year.

As Billy stood there, sadly gazing at the barren ground, the Devil came to him.

'Billy, do you think your Father loves you?'

'I should reckon He do.'

'Well I don't', continued the Devil, 'for if your Father loved you, Billy Bray, He'd give you a pretty yield of potatoes, as much as ever you want, and every one of them as big ʾs your fist.'

Billy couldn't stand this; he burst out:

'I used to have a personal acquaintance with you some years since, and I served you faithful as any poor wretch could; and all you gave me was nothing but rags to my back, and a wretched home, and an aching head, and no potatoes, and the fear of hell-fire to finish up with.

'And here's my dear Father in heaven. I have been a poor servant of His for thirty years. And He's given me a clean heart, and a soul full of joy, and a lovely suit of white that will never wear out, and He says He'll make me a king before He's done, and that He'll take me home to His palace to reign with Him for ever and ever.

'And now you come up here a-talking like that . . .'

But Billy said no more – there was no need to. He had resisted the Devil, and the Devil had already fled.

Of course Satan does not always come directly to a person; sometimes he makes his attack through one of his followers. This happened to Billy in January of 1867, while he was conducting meetings in Plymouth and Devonport. The meetings were lively, for those gathered there were rejoicing in the Lord.

But not everyone around felt the same about these gospel meetings. One man stopped Billy in the street and complained of the noise that came from the chapel during the services. Billy could be sharp, and he felt that this was a time for it.

'I do not mind who hears me. *You* are not ashamed to do your master's work out in the street, and I am sure we who love the Lord ought not to be ashamed to praise Him in the chapel.

'I do not fear you', Billy continued, 'nor your black-faced master. If I had hearkened to such as you I should have lost my best Friend long ago. My best Friend is the dear Lord. He has made me *glad*, and no one can make me *sad*. He has made me *shout*, and no one can make me *doubt*.'

6 *Billy's death*

BILLY was almost seventy-four years old now, and he was a sick man. Shortly before he died there were gospel meetings being held nearby, at Crantock. Though his body was now weak, Billy's spirit was still strong, so off he went to Crantock. He was not sorry he went:

'The dear Lord made the people very happy, and me happy with them. We could do nothing but praise, for the Spirit was poured out in such a wonderful manner. I was as happy as I could be and live. It was one stream of glory.'

As Billy struggled home from Crantock, he felt weak and tired. But a wonderful, fresh thought sprang into his mind:

'I think I shall be home to Father's house soon.'

Only once more did Billy leave his house. It was to visit his children in Liskeard. He became very ill, and at last sent for a doctor. When the doctor had looked him over, Billy asked, 'Well, doctor, how is it?'

'You are going to die.'

'Glory, Glory be to God!' Billy shouted in the doctor's ear. Then he asked pointedly; 'Shall I tell them in heaven you will be coming too?'

A few more days, and Billy had gone. But before he went he shouted just one word – 'Glory!'

DAVID BRAINERD

1 *Preparation*

NORTH AMERICA was a very wild country in the days of David Brainerd. It was a land where mountains were high, where forests were thick, and where rivers rushed down countless water-falls.

If it was wild in David's day, it was more so in the days of his great-grandfather, the Rev Peter Hobart. Mr Hobart had once lived in England, but when he and other ministers had been persecuted for their preaching, they had sailed to America in search of freedom.

Mr Hobart had a family of five boys, the second of whom was called Jeremiah. When Jeremiah grew up he became a minister like his father, and preached in various towns, the last being a place called Haddam. He was still able to attend church when he was an old man. When he was nearly eighty-five, however, he came from church one morning, and by the time the congregation gathered again that Sabbath evening old Jeremiah had been taken to join the church in heaven above.

Jeremiah's daughter became the mother of David Brainerd. In the town where the grandfather died, the grandson was born on the 20th April, 1718. David had four sisters and four brothers, and they were all happy for a time. There came a sadness, however, into their young lives. When David was nine, his father died. Five years later, a terrible sickness swept through the town of Haddam, and David's mother died too. So David and all his brothers and sisters were left alone while still young.

The sadness which David experienced made him a very serious young boy. Every day he prayed. He had seen his father and his mother die, and he wished to be prepared when his own time came. He also used to read the Bible. By the time he was a young man, he was so much in the habit of Bible-reading that he read ten chapters every day.

When he was nineteen he worked for a year on a farm, but he decided to give it up: he thought that he would rather be a minister than a farmer. Here, however, he met with a difficulty. As a minister, David would have to speak to others about faith in Christ – but he did not yet know what faith was himself!

David must have been fond of walking; he often used to go for long rambles while he turned over his problems in his mind. One morning he was walking through a lonely spot when a thought suddenly struck him. It was that, for all his reading of the Bible and praying, he was still a sinner at heart. At once he said to himself, 'Oh, I wish I had lived a better life'. But then he realized that however much better his life might have been, his heart would have remained the same. This was a terrible thought, and it shook him all over. It meant that God could not receive him to heaven. His best actions were still the actions of a sinner, and a holy God could never receive him on account of them.

The conviction that took hold of David's mind that day was so strong that he thought of little else for the next three days together. On the third day, he decided to go for another walk in the same direction. He was thinking dark thoughts about himself, and he was passing under a clump of trees that made the path dark too, when something happened. Suddenly his mind was filled with light from heaven. The sun began to set. The darkness of the woods grew deeper, and the big trees cast even denser shadows, but David stood still where he was. The thought that overwhelmed him now was that 'God is light'. When David had set out there had been light everywhere around him, but darkness in his heart. When he got home, there was darkness all around him but light in his heart. Where did he get that light? He got it from Christ. Christ had come to him, while he had walked in that dark grove. Christ had taken away the darkness of his sin and given him His righteousness. Now he knew what Christ says to us all: 'I am the light of the world'.

*

This experience, which David had in July, 1739, prepared him for being a real minister. Now that he knew Christ as his own Saviour from sin, he was ready to preach about Him to others, and the next three years were taken up with the usual studying which ministers do before they begin to preach.

David was now ready to preach – but to whom? This was a question he had often asked himself, but by now he had his answer. He would preach to the Red Indians, who knew nothing about the Saviour who was now so precious to him. Of course David was not like many of us, who have only met Red Indians in story books. As a child he had watched them in the woods near his home, and he had often met them on the streets of Haddam. So he already knew what the Indians were like, before he made his first preaching excursion about this time.

They were quite dark. Their faces were a dingy brown, and their eyes and hair were black like coal. Their hair was long and straight, but their eyes were specially noticeable. They were bright and restless. The reason was that they were used to looking everywhere at once, while travelling through the forest. Another effect of their frequent trekking was that their stride was longer than a white man's. This too was specially noticeable, as the average Indian was actually shorter than the average white man.

★

It was some time after David's first visit to the Indians before he returned to them as a regular missionary. In the meanwhile, he

D

made a trip to New York to meet a group of ministers. They represented a Missionary Society in Scotland, and they wished to meet David with a view to sending him as their missionary to the Indians. But first they had to examine him and hear him preach. David was very worried, and after he had preached he felt he had done very badly. The ministers must have thought differently, for they were sure that David was just the man they wanted. Yes, they decided, they would send him to work among the Housatonic Indians at Kaunaumeek. However, it was then winter, and David was not allowed to go into Indian country until the spring.

2 *Into the dark forest*

IN APRIL, 1743, David left the white settlement of Stockbridge and rode out into the forest. He was riding west to the Wild West. When he had gone about twenty miles, he came on a group of Indians. This was Kaunaumeek, and here David began his missionary work.

Life was very rough in Kaunaumeek. David was lodging with a Scotsman, whose wife spoke no English. The Scotsman's house was a rough log cabin, and David's share of it was a room which had no bed except some boards with straw spread on them.

David's food was not any more cheering than his lodging. He wrote to his brother John that he was living on 'hasty-pudding, boiled corn, and bread baked in ashes'. David did not complain, but his stay in this place was not very pleasant. For one thing, the cabin was a mile and a half from the nearest Indians. As the country was rough and David was making the journey twice a day he found this very tiring.

After a time, David left the Scotsman's house and lived with an Indian family. Certainly he was now nearer the Indians, but this arrangement was not very good either. David was used to living in a well-built, cosy house, and he must have found the Indian wigwam very draughty and cold.

When Indians built their houses, they never thought of erecting

a good, permanent building. Their only concern was to make something which could easily be taken down when they had to move on. The backbone of a wigwam consisted of three long branches which were spaced out at the bottom and tied together at the top. More branches were set around this structure, and then a covering of bark or deer-skin was wrapped round. There was a space in one side of the wigwam for people to get in, and a hole at the top for smoke to get out.

We can imagine that David was not very happy. The smoke from the open fire got into his eyes, and the rain and wind made him feel damp and cold. In the end, David had to build a little cottage

[91]

for himself. It was hard work, but once it was finished David found it was the best thing to have a place of his own. Here he could pray in peace. It was not just now and then that David prayed, nor for ten minutes at a time. He prayed every day, and sometimes he prayed all day. He loved the Indians, but he knew he could not convert them. This was why he spent so long asking God to do for them what he could not do by himself.

David liked to be alone to pray, but then he could not stay alone praying all the time. He had to go out to the Indians, to tell them about Jesus. This was not so easy as it might sound. It is one thing for us to take out a car and drive along a road: it was another thing for David to saddle his horse and ride through the forest. A car does not drive off on its own, but some mornings David could not find his horse; it had wandered off in the night! Also, the Indians were scattered through the woods in little groups. It was easy for them to travel; they were born in the woods and were expert at finding their way. But David was only a pale-face, and pale-faces often lost themselves in the Indian forest.

When a person was lost in the woods, he had reason to be afraid. There might be a rattle-snake near, or a pack of hunting wolves might pass by. At times, when David missed his way, he would manage to keep riding his horse all night. Sometimes, however, he was much too tired to ride and he would get off his horse and lie on the open ground. He knew it was dangerous to sleep where he was exposed to animals who could creep up and attack him before he wakened. But he knew also that the God who made all creatures was able to defend him, so he committed himself freely into His care, and found that the God who kept Daniel safe in the den of lions kept him too, in the forests of Kaunaumeek.

*

David prayed long and often for the conversion of the Kaunau-meek Indians, and sometimes he was encouraged to feel that God would answer his prayers. He continued to preach to them too. Sometimes he felt sad after preaching, but at other times he was very happy, when he felt that God was helping him in his work. One Sabbath like that was when he preached in the morning on the joys of heaven and in the afternoon on the miseries of hell. Afterwards, some Indians came up to him, earnestly asking to hear more about these things.

By March, 1744, David had been almost a year among the Indians of Kaunaumeek. There were really few Indians in the area, and David was by now wondering how long he should stay with them. Then he thought of a plan. There was a minister, John Sergeant, twenty miles away at Stockbridge; perhaps the Indians would be willing to go there to hear him preach. This would leave David free to visit other Indians who did not know about Jesus. But what if the people of Kaunaumeek were unwilling to leave their homes? When David explained things to them, however, they agreed to go. That these people were willing to give up their homes rather than lose the preaching which David had brought to them shows that the year he spent at Kaunaumeek had not been wasted.

David had gone out to Kaunaumeek like a sower with seed. He had sowed the seed of God's word in the rough ground of these Indians' hearts. It was therefore appropriate that, on his last Sabbath in Kaunaumeek, he should preach on the Parable of the Sower. He had so much to say on this that he preached from it in the evening as well as the morning. Even when the time came to end the evening address, David still had things to say, and hardly knew how to stop! Why did he preach so long? He tells us why: he 'longed God should take hold of their hearts'.

★

On the 14th of March, David rode away from Kaunaumeek. Travelling south-east, he arrived at New York in just a fortnight.

He then went on a little farther to Elizabeth Town, where he again met the ministers who had asked him to work among the Indians. While he was in this area, he was more than once invited to become the minister of congregations of white people. He saw there was a great need for the gospel to be preached among these white people, and he prayed that God would send out others who would preach to them. But for his part he felt he should go back to work among the Indians.

3 *The Forks of Delaware*

THE Forks of Delaware, where David was now to go, was far south-west of Kaunaumeek. Without much delay, David set off for his new out-post. He rode for mile after mile along the east side of the Hudson River, until he came to a place called Fish-kit. All the time he was praying that God would go with him to his new work. Then he crossed the Hudson River, and climbed up into an area called the Highlands, between the Hudson River and Delaware River. This was 'desolate and hideous country', but he eventually came out of it about twelve miles north of the Forks of Delaware.

When he arrived, David was very much cast down. The Indians seemed very scattered, and when he found groups of them he discovered that many were quite opposed to his message. The Indians had their reasons. When David told them he was going to speak about Christianity, the Indians thought: 'Oh, Christianity is the religion of the white man. The white man lies,

[94]

steals and kills worse than we ever did; his religion cannot be better than ours'. David had to admit that there was some truth in what the Indians said. Especially he thought with shame of how his own people had taught the Indians to get drunk. It was difficult to tell the Indians that those traders who had set them such a bad example were not Christians at all, and that Christianity must not be judged by them.

Another thing that set the Indians against David was their fear of being enslaved. The white people had been so mean to them at the beginning that they felt David must be coming to gather them together, only to make it easy to catch them and make slaves of them all. It was good that David had something to say in answer to this objection. He used to tell them that he was not sent to them by the people who took land from the Indians; rather he was sent among them by good people far, far away who had never set foot on any land of theirs.

A third matter that caused the Indians to oppose Christianity was their own religion. Apparently they used to believe in many gods, but after the white people came, the Red Indians decided that there were only three gods. One god had made the English, one god the negroes, and one god themselves. They thought of their god as superior to the god of the English, because their god had made them better than the English. When they used to watch the white settlers ploughing the ground and planting crops, they used to laugh to see them work so hard. They thought: 'It is all right for these poor white people to dig the ground like that: but we are above them. They have to work hard, but we can just lie on the ground and sleep, except that now and then we chase the deer'.

David was told what the Indians believed about the future by one very old Indian. He said that after death the soul went southward. (This was because the Indians, living in the north, were exposed to the cold; they thought that heaven must be in the south, as the climate was more pleasant there.) David then asked the old man if all souls went to heaven. He replied that only good souls were received into heaven, and that bad souls continually hovered around the walls of heaven, but could never get in.

So it was very difficult for David to teach the religion of the Bible to the Indians. They looked on an Indian becoming a Christian as we would look on a Christian becoming a heathen.

Although David was now settled at the Forks of Delaware, he had sometimes to leave his new home and make journeys to the south. But however much he enjoyed being with other Christians in southern towns, he never forgot his heathen Indians in the north. The 11th of June, 1743, for example, found David in a comfortable bed in Newark. He was far from the discomforts of his Indian home, but he was also far from being asleep. His thoughts flitted from the high northern mountains to the dark valleys that lay at their feet. Also the thunder of the rapids on the Delaware River echoed through his mind. 'Who can deliver them from their heathen darkness?' thought David. 'And who can arrest the flow of Indian souls, rushing on to a lost eternity?'

4 *By horse and canoe*

WHEN David returned to his own area, it was only to prepare for a longer journey: he was getting ready to travel to the west, where the Susquehannah Indians were. On the first of October he set out: he had with him another white man and two Indian chiefs, and also an interpreter. That night they lodged

DAVID BRAINERD

in a house, but the next day they left houses far behind, and faced a howling wilderness where no white man lived.

As they began to edge out into this wilderness, they soon realized that they were travelling in the most dangerous country that they had ever seen. There was no easy way through it: their path crept now up a steep mountain, and now it plunged to the bottom of a deep ravine. They had to struggle through bushy undergrowth where swamps lay, and to clamber over rocks. Towards evening, David's horse stumbled on some rocks and fell under him. He himself was not hurt, but his poor horse had broken her leg. There was nothing for it but to put the horse out of her pain and to continue the journey on foot. They halted at dark, and lit a fire to warm themselves and to scare wild beasts away. They also cut down some bushes to make a kind of shelter and lay on the ground to sleep. Winter was approaching, and the frost was very keen.

It was Friday when the little party broke clear from the wilderness to stand on the banks of the Susquehannah River. The place they had arrived at was called Opeholhaupung, and they found twelve Indian wigwams there. David went immediately to the village chief, spoke to him in a friendly way, and told him he had come to teach them about Christianity. At this the chief consulted with his men, and they told David that they would listen to him. When he had finished his first address, David asked if they would listen to him again. Again they held a consultation, and they said they would hear him at once. David was quite encouraged. After this the Indians told him they would listen to him for a third time the next day.

On the Saturday morning, David rose early to pray for these Indians who were now hearing the gospel for the first time. About noon he preached to them again, and afterwards he visited them in their homes. They had intended going on a hunting expedition on the Lord's Day, and David, as he went among them, tried to persuade them to put this off till the Monday.

The Indians agreed to this, so David preached to them on the Sabbath. On the Monday morning he visited the houses again, saying goodbye to his new friends. To his surprise, they said he must not go yet; they wished to hear him preach again! Gladly David waited, and when he had ended this last address he tried to answer their objections to Christianity.

The next morning the five visitors rose at four o'clock, and at five they were on their way. They travelled steadily eastwards for thirteen hours: then they made a fire and a shelter from the barks of trees. A little distance away, they could hear the howling of wolves.

By the time the party got home, winter was at the door. David had not yet made a proper house for himself, and he would need one very soon. The Indians helped him, and together they put up a strong hut.

★

During that winter David worked very hard, praying and preaching. Sometimes he was near to despair, as on one Sabbath morning in December. But he spent that afternoon praying that God would help him, and in the evening he felt much better. As he preached he was encouraged, for he saw tears on many brown faces.

★

When the spring of 1745 came, it was time to travel again. In little over a month, David rode six hundred miles. He was very tired after these journeys, but in May he thought once more of the Indians in the west whom he had visited the previous October. In the second week of May, therefore, he headed west again.

During this journey, he and his interpreter got a fright. They found that their horses were growing very weak, and at last they had to dismount. They concluded that the horses had eaten a poisonous plant in the woods, and all they could do was to go on foot themselves, and to drive their horses before them. That night they lay down in the open woods. It was difficult to sleep. A fierce north-easterly storm blew up: it seemed as if it would blast the trees off the mountains. David and his interpreter, already drenched to the skin, did not know what best to do. The rain was so heavy that they knew they could never start a fire. They had no shelter where they were, so they decided to move on in the hope of finding shelter ahead of them. In the mercy of God they did so, in the shape of a bark hut, and there they spent the night.

When they reached the Susquehannah River again, they

changed their horses for canoes. For a hundred miles they paddled down-river, contacting Indians of seven or eight distinct tribes. David preached to them by different interpreters, and although he was sometimes discouraged, he was also sometimes surprised at the willingness of the Indians to hear him.

At this stage of his journey, David experienced to the full the thrills and dangers of travelling by canoe. The Indian canoe was very light, so that it could move very quickly and was easily manoeuvred. It was made of birch bark, only about a quarter of an inch thick. Inside the canoe were some straps of wood which strengthened it, but the whole craft was so light that one man could easily lift it with one hand. Being so light, and having no keel, the canoe was easily upset, and many a wetting was experienced on a long trip. The Indians, however, were expert at avoiding disaster. They could shoot at great speed down foaming rapids, guiding their canoe all the time between dangerous rocks. They could even sail over waterfalls, and keep their canoe from capsizing at the bottom, though more commonly they carried their boats by land to avoid places where the water fell from any considerable height.

Having spent a fortnight on the river, David felt it was time to head back home. But getting there was not so easy. While he was riding through the wilderness he began to feel unwell. He had a terrible headache, and severe pain in his stomach. He knew that he was in the grip of a burning fever, but he had to keep on. For a while he thought that this journey would be his last, that he would perish in the wilderness. But at last he came on a clearing which was occupied by a hut where an Indian trader lived. Here he was allowed to stay, although the Indian could give him neither medicine nor proper food. Wonderfully, he recovered; in a week he was strong enough to ride home.

5 Encouragement

DAVID was travelling hundreds of miles over the most difficult terrain imaginable. He was very tired. However, news about him was also travelling through the dark forests, for his work had begun to bear fruit. Some Indians were now convinced that they should not worship idols, and this had become the talk of every Indian town.

David did not know this; in fact when he returned home he became depressed about his work. He had been over a year now at the Forks, and he had not seen the progress he had hoped for. Someone spoke to him about Crossweeksung, and he thought he should pay it a visit. It was about eighty miles south-east of the Forks, but David was told there were many Indians there.

On the 19th of June he arrived, and was immediately disappointed, for he found only two or three families in one place, with miles between each tiny settlement. Having come such a great distance, however, David could not leave without preaching to the few women and children he found. When he finished speaking, he noticed that the Indian women were preparing hurriedly to go on a journey. They were going off to visit their friends, ten or fifteen miles away, to announce that the Christian teacher had arrived. David stood amazed: clearly God had led him by means of a mistaken report to a place where the people had heard of him from others, and were eager to hear him for themselves.

Every day David saw his congregation grow. On the sixth day after his arrival a group of Indians came from a distance, and the missionary was asked to preach twice a day instead of once, so that they could make the most of his stay. With so many Indians living together, there might well have been difficulty in finding enough food for them all. But David found that God cared wonderfully even for this. Some of the men went only a few steps from the camp when they sighted three deer and killed them for food.

David was glad to have a congregation of fifty or sixty Indians. A greater encouragement, however, was the way these Indians listened. They listened in an awed silence; now and then they wept. They were afraid that the forgiveness of sins of which David preached might never be theirs. But soon it was time for the pale-face preacher to leave, and the Indians bade him a sad farewell.

If David thought his only encouragement was in the south, he was wrong. When he got home he was cheered to find that the interpreter and his wife were ready and willing to be baptized.

The story of David's interpreter is interesting. He is not, of course, the interpreter David had while at Kaunaumeek. While there, David had had the services of John Wauwaumpequnnaunt, and a very good interpreter he was. But John did not know the language of the south, so David had to look for another interpreter when he arrived at the Forks of Delaware. Moses Tinda Tautamy was the name of his new helper, and a great help he proved to be. For a time he seemed to be quite impressed by David's preaching, but it did not really take hold of him till he fell ill. Then the burden of his sins felt very heavy, and he was so distressed that he could not sleep. He described his feelings to David like this: He was trying to get to heaven, but there was a great mountain before him. He tried to press on, but he found his way blocked by a thorn hedge. He felt sure there might be hope, if he could only get round the hedge and struggle up the mountain, but he could not move. Then he said 'And now I thought that I must sink down to hell, now there was no hope for me, because I never could do anything that was good. If God let me alone never so long, and I should try never so much, still I should do nothing but what is bad.' Suddenly, however, it was as if a voice spoke to him, 'There is hope: there is hope.' After this, a great change appeared in his public speaking. Instead of merely translating David's words into the Indian language, Moses now became like a preacher himself. Sometimes when David had stopped speaking and gone back to his hut Moses felt that he must continue to preach about Christ to his fellow-Indians.

He had always served David well, but now he loved his work as never before. He loved David and he loved his message. He was never so happy as when translating for David the message of salvation through Jesus.

6 *Converts at Crossweeksung*

As you might expect, David could not long stay away from Crossweeksung, where he had felt so much of God's blessing on his work. He was back by the beginning of August, and was very much encouraged by what he saw. A real change had come over the lives of these Indians. When they now came together for a meal, they would not begin to eat till David arrived to ask a blessing for them. They also wept to think how they used to eat in honour of devils and had never till now given thanks to God for their food. When they were by themselves, they spoke constantly about the message which David was preaching to them. Moses was a great help to them in these discussions, for he was with them all the time.

David's message can be judged from his text on the 6th of August: 'Herein is love, not that we loved God, but that he loved us, and gave his Son to be the propitiation for our sins.' (1 John 4 : 10) His constant theme was the love of God, revealed in the death of Jesus Christ. Some of David's hearers had by now felt that love in their own hearts. When David asked them what they wished for now, they answered, 'We want Christ to wipe our hearts quite clean.' But many of David's hearers had not yet received the forgiveness of sin through Jesus, and these wept when David preached. They wept for fear they might never get what they now desired more than all the world.

★

Imagine you are in the camp of Crossweeksung on the 8th of August, 1745. In the morning, the bushes around the camp part, and some Indians who have been travelling since before dawn join the company. There are now about seventy Indians gathered together. Soon it is time for the morning service. The Indians gather close together and listen in a breathless silence. Now the silence is broken. It is an old man – a drunkard, a powwow (medicine-man) and a murderer – who is crying bitterly over his sins. The service ends, and David begins to go from tent to tent, speaking to the Indians one by one. And the effect is the same: whether David speaks to them together or individually, the Indians are immediately struck with a sense of their sinfulness. Some are so weak that they are forced to lie on the ground. Whether inside or outside, all weep as if they were alone in a dark forest with no-one near to see.

In the afternoon another newcomer arrives. But she is different. She has no concern for her own soul, and she only mocks to see others prostrate on the ground, pleading for mercy. She is very bold, this woman: she stalks up to the missionary's tent and speaks with him. David tells her he is soon to preach again, but her only response is a loud laugh.

When David begins to speak, however, she consents to listen with the rest. In a little while she is interested, and leans forward to hear what the preacher has to say. By the time he finishes, the stranger lies on the ground. In the afternoon, she had strength to march up to his tent and speak boldly with him, but now she cannot move. It is as if someone has knocked her down, though no one has touched her; it is as if she is deeply wounded, though her body bears no mark. She begins to cry. Some pity her, and gather round to ask what is wrong. She pays no heed, however, to any question, and continues to cry without a break. Then David comes and, standing over her, listens to what she is saying. 'Guttummaukalummeh wechaumeh Kmeleh Ndah' she says, over and over again. Moses translates, 'Have mercy on me, and help me to give Thee my heart'.

As darkness falls over the camp, some are kindling fires to cook the evening meal. Most, however, are too concerned about their souls to think of their bodies, while their believing friends take them by the hand, and ask them to give up their hearts to Christ.

7 Evil in the west

SOON David had to quit these scenes: it was time, he thought, to visit Susquehannah again. Before he left Crossweeksung, he gathered the people together, to tell them where he was going. He then made a request – he wanted the believers at Crossweeksung to pray for him and for the unbelievers at Susquehannah. Then he got astride his horse and left. As soon as the Indians had waved goodbye, they gathered together to pray: it was then about an hour and a half before sunset. The Indians were very earnest in prayer, and continued at it till they felt ready for sleep. Actually it was nearer time for rising than time for resting when they had finished. The hours had passed so quickly, they could not believe the hour when they broke up till they went out and saw the morning star at a considerable height.

David was by now well on his way to the Forks of Delaware: he wanted to visit there before he left for the west. It was on the 9th of September that David began his journey, and in four days he had travelled the one hundred and twenty miles to the Indian town of Shaumoking. This was a strange town, split in three. Part was on the east bank of the Susquehannah River, part on the west, and the rest was on an island in the middle. Here David found the chief of the Delaware Indians, and got permission to preach to his people. The chief was a kind man, but his people were rough and drunken. After two days, David gathered together a congregation of about fifty in a more sober part of the town, and preached to them. Two days later, David left Shaumoking and continued his journey by river.

About forty miles downstream he came in sight of a large inhabited island. It was called Juneauta Island, and here David beached his canoe. He was alone now, as Moses had had to leave him. In any case, Moses did not know the language spoken here. When David had obtained an interpreter, he proposed to preach. The Indians, however, had other plans. Dismayed, David discovered that they were all preparing for a big heathen sacrifice and dance. By the time darkness had fallen, about a hundred of them had come together and had lit a huge fire. The flames leapt high into the night sky, but apparently not high enough. The Indians had killed ten large deer as a sacrifice, and the fat from these deer they now threw on top of the bonfire. The dark island was lit as by lightning, and the Indians' whoops could have been heard miles away. Then they settled down to the business of dancing, and dance they did all through the night.

David was discouraged, but he thought he would get an opportunity to address these wild heathens when the Sabbath came. Even then, however, the Indians refused to listen to him for a moment, and David soon realized that they had something else in mind. There was a sickness among them, and they had asked their powwows to meet together to discover the reason for it.

Later in the day, David saw six conjurers gather into a group. He sat down about thirty feet away, and watched. What a sight these powwows were! Their hideous gear was matched only by their ridiculous gestures. Sometimes they stretched their arms full out, pushing away some unwanted thing. At other times they filled their mouths with water, and, striking their bulging cheeks, spurted it out in a fine mist. Now and again they beat their bodies with their hands, their faces twisted as if in anguish and their eyes rolling. Sometimes they just danced around, singing and howling, grunting and puffing.

Altogether David thought that if anything in the world were suited to raise the devil, this was it. For about three hours this show went on; then the powwows broke up, apparently having failed to find an answer to their problem. Seizing his opportunity, David stepped up to the Indians, trying to speak to them about Christ. But it was no use: they scattered, leaving him very much alone.

David may have felt that now he had seen his most frightening sight, but Juneauta Island held another horror for him. One day a figure began to dance towards him, covered from top to toe in hairy bear skin. Its face was hidden behind a hideous wooden mask, half pale, half dark, and in its paw the creature held a rattle made of tortoise shell, which it waved in time to its dance. David could not but shrink back, even though he knew it was no more than a man in disguise. He spoke to this 'figure' about Christianity, but found that he too was a kind of missionary who was going among his fellow-Indians, trying to revive among them the ancient beliefs and practices of their pagan forefathers.

David was to visit the Susquehannah River once more, under happier circumstances, but meanwhile he left it with a very heavy heart.

8 *What grace can do*

D URING his trip in the west, David had been depressed by a feeling of helplessness. When he got back to Crossweeksung, however, he was uplifted by a sense of God's power. The Indians there had been just as heathen as those at Susquehannah, but by the grace of God they had been totally changed. Here is the story of two of these Indians.

★

David had first noticed one of them because she was out-of-doors, even though it was December. He had been surprised because it was night time; he was even more surprised to see sweat pour from her face, as she looked up in the cold night air. She was praying very earnestly, and afterwards she explained her feelings to him: 'ME try, me try save myself: last my strength be all gone – could not me stir bit further. Den last, me forced let Jesus Christ alone; send me hell if He please.' Although her thoughts were very sad at this time, this woman soon discovered the truth of Christ's words: 'Him that cometh to me I will in no wise cast out'. Her feelings then were described in the words: 'Me grad (glad) desperately'.

Not long after, she came to David again. By her face he could see that she was now very happy. But she had a question to ask – Was it not true that David had been sent among them by good people from far away? He replied: 'Yes, by the good people of Scotland'. The woman then explained that she had felt so much love to these people the evening before that she had not stopped praying for them all night.

★

The other instance is that of the old conjurer already referred to in chapter 6. This old man actually used to live near the Forks of

Delaware; it was there that he first met David. For a year he now and then attended David's preaching, but three things kept him from coming more often. First, he was a drunkard, and he knew that the Bible was against him for this. Secondly, he was a powwow, dealing in satanic magic. This was a great worry to David, because this man's influence as a magician kept many others from believing the Bible. When David spoke of Christ's miracles as showing Him to be God, the people merely said that this powwow was able to do these miracles too. The third thing that made the old man stop coming near David for a time was that he had murdered a young Indian. When David did get a hold of him he told him how his sins might be forgiven for Christ's sake, and this encouraged the murderer to listen to the gospel.

On the 21st of July, he was among the crowd who saw Moses Tautamy and his wife baptized. This was of course the first baptism he had ever seen, and he was deeply impressed. So much so, in fact, that he left the Forks ten days later and followed David down to Crossweeksung, where he heard him preach on the 8th of August. After this experience, when he 'felt the word of God in his heart' his power of conjuring utterly left him. During the whole of that autumn and winter his mind was full of concern about his sins. On the 1st of February, 1746, while hearing David preach again, his fears reached a new height. He trembled for hours together, afraid he was dropping into hell.

Then, as suddenly as the storm broke over this old man's head, it was gone. David saw this at once, and asked him how things were. 'It is done, it is done, it is all done now', he replied. Asked what he meant, he explained: 'I can never do any more to save myself: it is all done for ever. I can do no more. My heart is dead; I can never help myself.' David then asked what was to happen to him. He replied, 'I must go to hell'. David asked if he thought it right that he should go to hell. 'Oh, it is right. The Devil has been in me ever since I was born. I have always served the Devil, and my heart has no goodness in it now, but is as bad as ever it was.'

[109]

Although this man seemed so sure he was lost, his calm bearing betrayed a secret hope hiding in his heart. He often used to ask David when he would preach next, and David would ask him why he wanted to hear preaching when his heart was dead, and he was lost. He would reply, 'I love to hear you speak about Christ . . . I would have others come to Christ, if I must go to hell myself.'

Days passed, and then, as David was preaching again, the old man began to weep afresh. But this time it was different: his tears flowed from the joy that welled up in his heart. Christ had met the old murderer, taken away his fear of hell, given him a sure hope of heaven, and was not this good reason to weep for joy?

After this he seemed to follow David wherever he went. On one occasion, up at the Forks of Delaware, another old conjurer threatened to bewitch the missionary and his followers. After a short time the converted conjurer stood up and said: 'You have no power to hurt them, not so much as to touch one of them. I was once a conjurer as great as you are. But as soon as I felt in my heart that word which these people love, my power of con-juring left me, and so it would you, if you once felt it in your heart.' So, as was true of the Apostle Paul, this old man preached the faith which once he destroyed.

9 Crossweeksung: the church established

WHEN David had come to Crossweeksung first, in March, 1745, he had not found ten Indians living there. Now, a year later, around a hundred and fifty had gathered to live in that part. Even on week-days David held many services, and those on Sabbath began about half-past-eleven, and hardly stopped until after seven at night.

The Indians usually lived in small groups, depending for food on what they could hunt in the forests. Now that so many had come together, they had to look for a steadier source of food. The Indians had never cultivated the soil, but David explained to them that they would need to do so now. The ground at Crossweeksung was poor, so they began to make a clearing in the trees about fifteen miles away: they had to hurry, as the planting season was near. David prayed with them for a blessing on their work. Such prayer was needed; there were white men who would grudge good land to the Indians, and might try to drive them off it.

Thus David cared for the bodily needs of the church at Crossweeksung. Of course, he cared for their spiritual needs far more. One matter that occupied his mind in the spring of 1746 was that the Indian church had never remembered the Lord's death in the special way appointed in his Word: now was the time to do so.

On the 27th of April the Lord's Table was spread in these dark forests for the first time. Although some were away who could have attended, twenty-three Indians remembered the Lord's death that day. Afterwards David went among his people to see how they felt, and noticed one thing above all else. They had such love to one another! David knew that if the heathen Indians were noted for anything, it was for quarrelling and fighting. What must his thoughts have been that day, as he saw love flow so freely between these Indian Christians? Surely he felt nearer to heaven than he had ever done before!

This was the first time that David served the Lord's Supper to his Indian people, but it was not the last. In July thirty-one Indians sat at the Table, after David had spoken on the words, 'I am the Bread of Life' (John 6 : 35). Again the occasion was marked by the tenderness and affection of those who had until so recently been in the grip of heathenism and hatred.

In July, David more than once spoke of his intention to visit Susquehannah again, so that the believers at Crossweeksung could pray with him for the success of the trip. On the eleventh of August, he preached from the words, 'And when they had prayed, the place was shaken.' (Acts 4 : 31). In a measure, the truth preached was fulfilled before the preacher's eyes, and the Holy Spirit was evidently with the little church at Crossweeksung as He had been with the disciples at Jerusalem. Also as David explained Psalm 110, Psalm 2, and Psalm 72, the Spirit lifted up the hearts of those present to see by faith the coming of the Saviour's kingdom. It was a very precious time for the missionary, as he saw the faces of converted heathens alight with the hope that their still heathen brothers would be converted too. The next day, David set off with six of the men whom he thought most suitable to help him in his task.

In about a week the party had arrived at Shaumoking. David called again to see the chief of the Delawares, while his Indian friends went out to meet the people of the town. On their second day in Shaumoking, David preached to a large number of Indians. When he had finished speaking, the Indians from the east spoke to their heathen brothers to support what the preacher had just said.

David's plan for this trip was to ride north along the banks of the Susquehannah, instead of travelling to the south. In the beginning of September he got as far north as The Great Island, but here he had to stop. Sickness was widespread among the Indians, and David himself felt weak and ill. He travelled faster than the Indians, however, as he was on horseback and they on foot. One night when they were on their way back to Shaumoking David had to get off his horse in the early evening, being overcome with weakness. He lay there alone in the forest, and wearied for his Indians to come. They caught up with him about ten o'clock, and found him asleep, though without fire or food.

This last journey was much more encouraging than earlier ones had been. At times the Susquehannah Indians would accompany the visiting party for miles, hanging on to hear more of the gospel. Sometimes on the homeward journey David came across groups who would beg him to stay and preach. David would have loved to do so, but he found he could not wait. He had no strength left for preaching, and he wondered at times if his strength would be enough to take him home.

By the end of September, however, he did get home again. How happy he was to find his Indians met in a house for prayer! Before going to rest David prayed too, and many wept to hear how God had answered their prayers for the success of his mission in the west.

★

David was now an ill man: he did not know how long he might live to care for his Indian church. It was natural therefore that he should wish to remember the Lord's death among them again at Crossweeksung, before he was taken from them. So it was announced, not only there but also at the Forks of Delaware, that the first Sabbath of October would be the day for one other communion service. David mentions in his Diary that forty-seven Indians up at the Forks had made a good profession of Christianity, so some of these doubtless took this opportunity to have fellowship with the church at Crossweeksung.

As the time approached, David was afraid that his health would break, but he prayed for strength, and his prayer was answered. On the chosen Sabbath he preached from John 1 : 29, 'Behold the Lamb of God, which taketh away the sin of the world.' Afterwards he handed the symbols of bread and wine to around forty Indians. Crossweeksung that day was like the city of Samaria, where the preaching of Philip had been received: 'there was great joy in that city' (Acts 8 : 8). The preacher's strength, however, was spent, and he had to be helped the little distance to his hut. As he lay in pain and weakness, the camp of Crossweeksung was not silent, but the noise that David heard was only such as cheered his heart. From hut after hut, until near midnight, he heard the voice of a living church: the sound of Indian prayer and Indian praise.

10 'Into peace'

THE days that followed were difficult days in which David's body was pained, in which it broke his heart to see his Indians hover hopefully around his door, wondering if they would hear his voice again. One Sabbath he felt stronger and the Indians crowded in to listen to him preaching from his bed. It was not easy to hear him: his voice was so low and weak. But the preaching was powerful, and many were in tears.

Before the end of 1746 David had gained a little strength, and he came to a decision. He would leave Crossweeksung, and see whether a change of air would improve his health. Of course he did not ride in the way he used to do: now he went very slowly, and leaned on his horse's neck. As dark Indian eyes watched the figure which was fast merging with the shadows of the forest, there was a lump in every throat and an emptiness in every heart.

Once he reached Elizabeth-town, David was well cared for: he was nursed at the home of a local minister. Here he spent the rest of the winter: sometimes he was better and at other times very weak. When March came round he had a little strength, and he knew how to spend it: he would go and see Crossweeksung once again.

He arrived in the early morning, and visited the Indian wigwams. At ten o'clock he called the Indians together and gave out a psalm, which he explained, once more giving out the bread of life in the word of God. Then they sang the Psalm together, and David prayed. At eleven o'clock the Indians at Crossweeksung saw David Brainerd for the last time.

★

Although it was known that David had consumption, he was still advised to ride: doctors then had no other advice to give to a man in his condition. So David rode on, while his strength lasted. He came to New York, and turned north to his own country. He was young to be coming home like this, a dying man; he had just passed his twenty-ninth birthday.

Near the end of May he rode on still farther, and reached Northampton, Massachusetts. This was the home of Jonathan Edwards, the great preacher who published David's Diary after his death. (You can still buy David's Diary, and read about his life in his own words.) It was here, in the house of Jonathan Edwards, that David spent the closing months of his brief life. These were days of great weakness, but at times David felt and saw the power of God as never before. From his death-bed David foresaw the Saviour coming in His Kingdom, and that sight made him glad. Now he was sure that the work of God would go on, until His Spirit was poured out on all nations.

The day before his death he was delighted to see his brother John again. He had been away at Crossweeksung, and brought David news of the Indians whom he loved.

He was to succeed David at Crossweeksung, so he wanted to

hear any advice his dying brother had to give. David was soon too weak to speak, but warm tears showed that love still flowed in his heart – love to John and love to the Indians whom they both served. David longed for death, most of all because he knew that in heaven he would serve God without sin. The last entry in his diary reads: 'Oh come, Lord Jesus, come quickly. Amen.' About six o'clock on the morning of the 9th of October, 1747, David's prayer was answered.

★

A few of the converted Indians had died before their loving pastor. His work thus went to heaven before him, and there were Indians to meet him around the throne. How they must have welcomed him into the throng of the redeemed, to sing God's everlasting praise!

ROBERT ANNAN

1 *A prodigal son*

H IS young friends used to call him 'The Water-Dog', for Robert Annan was a strong and fearless swimmer. Even when snow lay on the land, and frost was in the air, Robert would dive into sea or river to bathe.

He kept wild company; he liked to be with those who were strong and restless like himself.

If you had been around Robert's house about dawn, you might have wondered why a string was hanging from a bedroom window. If you had stood to watch, you would have soon seen why. Robert's young companions would come along and pull the string. The string was tied to his ankle – a device to waken and bring him out before the household was astir. Then the lively crowd would run to play in field or wood. As far as Robert was concerned, however, all this activity was to come to a sudden halt.

Imagine the inside of a Dundee prison in the 1840's. Robert Annan was now a youth, and he did not need to imagine what a prison cell looked like – he was seeing it for himself. At the age of fourteen he had been apprenticed to a merchant. Then he had left that, and worked for a time with his father, who was a mason. He began to learn the mason's trade, but he began to learn other things as well. He learned bad habits: he began to drink and brawl. And this was where that ended – within the four small walls of a prison cell. He remembered these four walls for long afterwards; they were almost all he saw for three whole months.

★

When he came out of prison, Robert promised to change his ways. His father listened to him, and took him at his word. He wanted to help his son make a new start in life, so he gave him money and sent him to America. On the voyage, the ship went down and Robert escaped death by a hair's breadth. But this brush with death left no impression. When he reached land he went as hard as ever in the ways of sin. One night, in a wild mood, he threw himself across a railway line and slept. But the Lord pitied him more than he had pitied himself, and kept him from danger till the morning.

Soon his money was spent, and his clothes worn out. Destitute, he wandered north till he crossed the border into Canada. It was winter, and what a winter! He almost perished, as he searched vainly for someone who would employ him. At last one man had pity on him. He was a farmer who reared pigs, and for a time Robert fed them.

Finding no proper work, Robert decided to join the Hundredth Regiment of the British army. Soon afterwards, the regiment left Canada for England, and camped at Aldershot. In the army, strangely enough, he met kind Christians. Their influence, together with the discipline of army life, restrained Robert's spirit for a time.

However, one day there was no Robert Annan to answer the roll-call at Aldershot. At the same time, there was what appeared to be a tramp trudging across neighbouring fields. Disguised in old clothes, with a boot on one foot and a shoe on the other, Robert was deserting.

At last he reached London, but what could he do now? He had no money, and he was lost in the great city. In the end he joined a company of marines, and soon found himself on the way to Gibraltar.

This was too much. Part of his reason for leaving the army had been that his regiment was assigned to Gibraltar, and Robert had no wish to go there. Yet he was now being taken there by the navy. Robert's ship, the 'Edgar', anchored off the Rock, and from the ship's deck Robert could see some of his old comrades on duty there. Fear began to fill his mind. What if he was recognised as Robert Annan the deserter? Every time he met a soldier he feared his time had come. Then he could stand it no longer – he gave himself up.

Of course, deserters received severe punishment. Still smarting under it, Robert wrote to his parents. His father thought, 'Surely this time Robert will be truly sorry for his wayward life'. He posted money to Gibraltar, and obtained his son's release from the navy. Soon, the door of that Dundee home swung open again to receive the wandering son.

2 *Saved by grace*

IF Robert felt any shame on his return, he soon lost it. He felt he had become a new man, and he did not think too much about the past. He had changed his life, he thought, and had mastered his evil habits. He felt proud of that.

He was so sure that he was no longer a drunkard that he went one night to take a friend away from a place where he was drinking with other men. This friend said he would go with Robert, but on one condition. Robert must prove that he had really changed by drinking a glass with the others – just one glass. Robert did so. But not just one. He had been used to drinking all night – how could he stop at one glass? Instead of taking his

E

friend away from wicked companions, the friend drew Robert into their company. And there he stayed for the evening: drinking, drinking, drinking.

In the morning, the memory of the night before came upon him like a nightmare. He saw his hopes, his boasts, his ambitions lie all around him. He had tried to save himself – *and had failed.*

At that time (1860–61) gospel meetings were being held in a large hall in Dundee, and many souls were being saved. Robert thought it out – should he go? Yes, he would go along and hear what the preacher had to say. But the message he heard did not ease Robert's anguished mind. He had come with a feeling of sadness: he was now leaving with a feeling of desperation. On the steps he paused. A number of others who had attended the meeting remained behind to ask about the way of salvation. Could *he* wait? He had recently been sure of salvation in his own strength – could he now humble himself to ask others how to be saved? The thought of a judgment to come spurred him back up the steps to the big hall door. But it slammed in his face. Oh! What did this mean? Would he be shut out from salvation for ever?

The clocks of Dundee struck midnight as Robert knocked anxiously on the door of a minister's manse. The minister got a fright. This big man on his doorstep looked so wild! But he took him in, and then he noticed something. The 'big man' was quaking with fear. He had come to ask one thing, one all-important question: 'What must I do to be saved?' (Acts 16 : 30). The minister did for Robert Annan what Paul had done for the Philippian jailor at the same hour of the night. He pointed him to salvation in the Lord Jesus Christ. The man in Philippi had got relief at midnight, but not our man in Dundee. After hearing the minister for a time, he walked out again into the night.

As Robert left the manse behind him, a purpose formed in his restless mind. There was a hill, called the Law, overlooking the town, and Robert would climb that and pray there. He had often gone there as a carefree child, but when he approached it as an anxious man he could not find it. 'I could see no hill,' he said; 'the mountain of my sin rose before my eyes, and the wrath of God like a mist blinded me.'

As soon as this plan failed, other plans thrust themselves into Robert's mind. But in the end he went home. He did not enter the house, but rather climbed into a hay-loft, and lay down. For

thirteen hours he lay there, pleading with God for mercy. Light came in the morning for the outside world, but no light arose in Robert's mind.

He was alone in the loft; he had no company but his own cries. His parents and sister, wondering where he was, went searching for him in the morning. Then they heard him, and climbed up to join him in the hay-loft. They persuaded him to enter the house, but not to eat or drink – he had no mind for that. Nor could he sleep. For three days he did not eat, drink, or sleep.

At the end of three days, alone in that darkened room, Robert was listening. He hoped he would hear a voice from heaven saying, 'Robert, your sins are all forgiven'. Then he did hear something. But it was not a voice from heaven: it was the voices of two men who had come to see him. They did not know what he had been thinking before they came, but they spoke as God directed them.

'Robert, you are looking for a sign from heaven. You think that if you heard a voice assuring you of salvation, or felt some strange thing within you, you would believe and rest on Jesus. God gives you his word: will you not rest on *that*? "Believe on the Lord Jesus Christ and thou shalt be saved." Jesus says, "Him that cometh to me I will in no wise cast out".'

These two ministers had then to leave Robert. But what they had said remained with him. After another three days, the words which they quoted came to mean everything to him: 'Him that cometh to me *I* will in no wise cast out'. He came, and his darkness gave way to light, and the burden fell from his back. He came, and he was 'in no wise cast out'. He came, and he knew he was received as certainly as if he had heard a voice from heaven say, 'Robert, your sins are all forgiven.'

3 *Serving Christ*

THAT night there was to be a meeting in one of the Dundee halls. It was not the kind of meeting to which Robert had recently gone to hear the gospel. It was the opposite – it was a meeting at which a man was going to speak against the Bible, through which Robert had that day come to know his Saviour.

You might have seen Robert, then, on the night of his conversion, making his way with others to that hall. But he stopped at the door; he did not go inside. He was not wishing to hear a man speak against the Lord Jesus Christ, and he wished that others, too, would not be led astray by him. So he stood at the hall door and gave out tracts to those who were going in. All who knew his past expressed surprise – wasn't this the young man who used to lead others into drunken brawls? But even Robert's face witnessed to the great change that had since taken place. He was radiant with the joy of salvation.

From that time, Robert put his whole will and strength into seeking lost souls for Christ. There were other young men in Dundee of a similar spirit, and Robert soon became their leader. They met once a week for prayer and Bible study. Then they discussed their plans for the week. They would visit the sick and dying, they would hold meetings for prayer and preaching in poor areas. In short, they would spend their spare time bringing the good news of salvation to those who needed it most.

At that time, Robert seemed to be everywhere around Dundee. He worked during the day as a mason. In the evening he was preaching at some street corner. If you did not see him there, you might find that he had gone to the country to preach the gospel in some village hall.

He was always busy, but he never grew tired of the work. It grew on him so much that sometimes he would stop his work as a mason and use his tiny savings to go on a fortnight's preaching tour. The first of these tours took him round Fife. One evening when he stood up to speak he reminded his hearers that he had previously been among them to entertain them. He had sung silly songs and acted the fool. 'I have come to you on a different errand this time', he said, 'and will sing to you other songs. At that time I was making merry on the way to hell, and I was helping you to make merry in the same way; but now I am happy in Jesus, and on the road to heaven, and I have come to try to persuade you to go with me.'

Robert met with real encouragement in his preaching, for some souls were evidently born again. About 1862 he became a full-time missionary, and worked in more than one area of the north-east. Here, he did not find things so easy. He found that men did not wish to hear about eternity, nor about being born again. His hearers sometimes scoffed at his message. Not content with that, some even took hold of him and handled him roughly. What a trial for a man who, if not restrained by grace, could have knocked his attackers lifeless! But instead of defending himself with his fists, Robert went away to pray. He was discouraged by the opposition to his preaching, and even began to wonder if God were with him or not. A few days afterwards, he had his answer. A young man stood up at the close of a meeting, but this time it was not to hurl abuse at the speaker. It was to say that God had visited and saved his soul.

In 1864 Robert returned to Dundee. He took up his work as a mason again, but gave every spare moment to the service of God. Sometimes he was at his work by four o'clock in the morning. Instead of resting when he came home in the evening, he took his Bible with him to the street and preached. Sometimes, as before, he would go to the country to preach. Of course, going to the country in those days did not mean for Robert a pleasant run in bus or train – he walked. If he was short of time, he ran.

4 *A street meeting*

EVERY Sabbath morning and evening, Robert preached at Fish Street, or Couttie's Wynd, or Tyndal's Wynd. (A wynd was a narrow, back-street lane.) Even in winter he would be there, knee-deep in snow. Of course it rained, too; once his Bible got so wet he could not turn the leaves. The people in these Dundee wynds could not foretell the weather. But one thing they could be sure of. So long as Robert Annan was alive, he would be there to preach to them every Lord's Day.

But come and see for yourself what a Dundee Wynd was like. The street is so narrow, and the buildings so high, you cannot see the sky. If it is ever seen here, it is rarely blue. It is grey or brown, discoloured by the smoke and fog of the city. Someone's washing hangs stretched between one side of the lane and the other. Drunken men lie in the gutter, mumbling endlessly. No one understands what they say; no one cares. And the children! They are half-clothed, though it is winter. They dart in and out of the dark closes, playing to keep warm.

Then something draws attention to the end of the Wynd. It is the sound of singing. No, not the song of a drunkard, but the sound of a hymn. The voice is not sweet, but it is loud and hearty. It belongs to Robert Annan. A little crowd gathers, as Robert begins to pray. He prays as a real child of God who leans with all his weight on his heavenly Father's arm:

'O Father, we are come out here to ask Thy blessing and speak to poor sinners about salvation. Give us Thy Holy Spirit, that we may speak and hear as for eternity. Fill our hearts with Thy love, and may we all feel it good to be here. Give us a word to speak to

these precious souls. These are poor things trembling in the cold
of this cold world; oh, take them in and warm them at Thy fire.
If they only felt Thy love they would be warm enough. Do not let
the Devil spoil our meeting. Take the prey out of his hands this
night, and give us a blessed season, for Jesus' sake, Amen.'

When you open your eyes, scan the pool of faces around. These
are the faces of coal-heavers, shore-porters, fish-wives, beggars
and loafers – the usual hearers.

Robert begins his address. His text is, 'Peace with God'. He
speaks about false peace, then goes on:

'Peace with God is the great thing. If you have that peace, God
is your friend, and you need not care who is with you, or who is
against you. If you have peace with God you will have peace with
yourself, and will have peace in your conscience. Oh, how sweet

it is to lie down and sleep at peace with God! It was this that made Paul and Silas sing in a dungeon at the hour of midnight. It was this peace that made the martyrs so brave that they went to death as if they were going to a marriage, and sang for joy in the midst of the flames. This peace would support and cheer you in affliction; and it is the softest and safest pillow for a dying bed. If you were to lay your weary soul on this pillow and die tonight, you would awake in the arms of Jesus. Truly, it is a peace that passeth all understanding. Will you have it?'

The crowd has stood still around the preacher, but now there is some movement at the edge. A policeman, urged by a wine-seller, has come along to break up the meeting. Robert has to stand off the chair he used for a pulpit, and go away. The people are not pleased; they know he comes because he loves them. Someone mutters, 'That's aye the wye. They wud prosekeete Christ Himsel' if He cam doon the closs.'

5 The Master first

ROBERT had married in 1862. One day his wife said to him, 'You might get your portrait taken for five shillings'. But Robert replied, 'My dear Jeannie, I would to God I had five shillings to buy gospel tracts with for poor sinners.' Another time, Jeannie spoke about her man's hat. It was somewhat out of shape, as he had a habit of holding it in his hand while preaching. She thought he should try to get a new one. But Robert thought little of hats. 'It will do me very well, Jeannie. What I want is, not a good hat, but a good heart. Let us not seek the world's braws

[129]

(good things). What I want is heaven's braws – the grace of God. The grace of God, Jeannie, and to help others to get it.'

★

And help others to get it he did. Night and day he spent his strength in love to sinners, until his death at the early age of thirty-three.

About six months before he died, Robert's love for others more than for himself was specially proved. He was offered a job in Glasgow, and told this would bring him a higher wage. A working man in the 1860's was very poor, and a little extra money would be very useful. But Robert decided:

'No: God is blessing my poor endeavours here just now, and I will not go. Saving souls is better than making money.' God honoured Robert for this decision. From that time till his death, his meetings were crowded and many souls received a blessing.

★

At the onset of the last winter that Robert saw, he came home one night shivering with cold. Jeannie remarked that his coat had worn very thin, and said he would need a new one before winter really set in. 'Well, Jeannie', he said, 'we'll tell the Master about it, and maybe He will give me a new coat.' That night the new coat was mentioned in prayer at the Annan's house. The next day a letter arrived from an unknown friend, containing enough money for a new coat.

A similar incident happened after Jeannie mentioned to Robert that others seemed able to give their children a holiday. This touched him. 'Well', he said, 'perhaps the Lord will send us the means, and we'll get a day out.' The next day that 'means' arrived. Robert arranged for a family outing, then noticed that the Lord had sent more than enough for the little holiday.

There was enough over to buy some tracts. So Robert himself spent the day at his favourite occupation – seeking souls for Christ.

★

During those last six months of Robert's short life, he was used in the awakening of many souls. This was true both of his work in the open air and of the meetings he held in a large unfurnished room which was granted for the purpose.

One young man was just leaving one of Robert's meetings when he felt the preacher's strong hand on his shoulder, and heard a voice in his ear: 'Let us walk home together'. In a moment they were walking down the street, and Robert was asking:

'How is it with your soul?'

'Well enough', was the reply.

'And what is your reason for thinking you are saved?' Robert continued. The young man had given an easy answer to the first question, but to the second he could return no answer at all. He began to feel uneasy, and wished he could escape from the preacher's company. Soon they came to a well, and Robert turned to speak to some women there. This was his chance, but somehow the young man could not run away. Then Robert was by his side again, asking more unwelcome questions.

'Do you ever pray?'

'Yes.'

'What do you pray?'

'I pray the Lord's prayer.'

'Do you ever pray for a clean heart?'

'No.'

'Then you never saw your need of a new heart?'

'No.'

Before they parted, Robert had got his man to promise that he would pray that very night for a new heart. But the promise was broken. As the man lay in bed trying to sleep, the broken promise rankled in his mind. There was nothing for it but to rise and pray as Robert had told him to do. But it was not just a matter of fulfilling the promise and falling asleep. Sleep was now far from him. He had refused to pray before sleeping; now he found himself praying all night and getting no sleep! In the morning, he searched out the man he would have run from the previous evening. This concern ended in his conversion.

Of course, Robert Annan would almost certainly have prayed for hours for that man after speaking to him. Often whole nights were spent in prayer like this. And, whatever happened on other nights, every Saturday night was wholly spent in prayer.

Another young man who attended a meeting which Robert addressed felt sure that the preacher must secretly have discovered all his sins. Actually, Robert knew nothing of this man, but of course the Lord did. He had used Robert's message to convince the man of sin. After a time of concern, the man began to despair of ever finding salvation.

While speaking to the young man one day, Robert took a letter from his pocket. Robert had written it himself, and he asked his friend if he believed that the letter told the truth. He replied that he did not believe Robert would write what was not true. 'Well', said Robert, 'it appears that you can believe my words, but you cannot give God credit for speaking the truth. God promises to forgive your sins and save you, if you but trust Him; and you will not.' In time, what Robert said was blessed to this man, and he became a joyful believer in the Lord Jesus.

To yet another young man who had been convinced of sin under his preaching, Robert said:

'You are casting your anchor in the ship's hold, instead of throwing it overboard; you are seeking peace in your own heart, instead of looking out to Christ for it.' This helped the man to understand that salvation is all of grace. He, too, soon blessed God for sending to him one who helped him to rejoice in the Lord.

6 The last week

WEDNESDAY, 24th July, 1867 was a calm day. I suppose there were a few rafts afloat that day in Dundee harbour, but our interest centres on one of them. Robert Annan was standing on it, alone.

And yet he was not alone. Of course, the Lord Jesus is always with those who believe in Him, but there are times when they feel His presence in a special way. This was one of those times. The Saviour's presence was so near to Robert, it was like the dawning of eternal happiness. He wondered if he were already in heaven.

But the raft shook gently and Robert knew that he was still on earth. He said to himself, 'I am not yet in heaven, but perhaps I will be there soon.' To others he said, 'Jesus came to me on the water, and I thought that I was home. Do not wonder if you hear some strange thing about me one of these days.'

★

The next Sabbath morning Robert went along as usual to the police and asked permission to speak on the street. As he and a friend walked away, he said, 'I've got my ain place ance mair, Willy.'

The meeting at Couttie's Wynd that morning began with the hymn, 'For ever with the Lord'. In his address, Robert referred to his experience on the previous Wednesday.

'Dear people, I cannot tell you how happy I was last Wednesday morning down there upon the water, when the Lord showed me His glory. If you but tasted these joys, you would wonder at your present foolishness in putting Christ away from you. I may never have another opportunity of speaking to you. I may be in heaven before next Sabbath.'

That meeting was early in the morning, and Robert preached in different parts of the city till late that Sabbath night. Then he went home, exhausted but unspeakably happy.

★

The next Wednesday morning Robert rose at four o'clock, and prayed for a long time. When he was going out of the house he carried a piece of chalk in his hand. He wrote DEATH on the gate. Outside the gate he paused again. He stooped, and wrote ETERNITY on the pavement. Then he turned and went off to work down by the harbour.

Around mid-day he heard a cry. An eleven-year-old boy had

fallen into the water, and was struggling for his life. Robert plunged in to save him.

People gathered on the shore to watch. Perhaps they had seen Robert save folk from drowning before; he was famous for it. In fact, he had once saved two lives separately on the same day. That Wednesday seemed just like one of those days. They saw Robert reach the sinking child, and turn round for the shore. They waited to receive him.

But he did not come. The current was at that time very strong, and even his strength was not enough to overcome it. The watchers were frozen to the spot. Then they ran. They got two boats and launched them.

They were too late. The boy, whom Robert had held up, was safe. But Robert had gone down.

★

When Robert Annan died, it was as if Dundee itself had lost a brother. He had been taken for granted while alive. Now that he had gone, everyone spoke of his wonderful life, and of his tragic death.

A day or two later, a vast crowd gathered before the tiny house where the young man had lived. To begin the funeral service, a minister prayed outside the house. He stood on a flag-stone with letters chalked on it. Those who were near could read, 'ETERNITY'.

On the Sabbath following, a funeral sermon was preached in the church of which Robert had been a member. The text was, 'And Enoch walked with God, and he was not, for God took him' (Genesis 5 : 24). A wave of sadness swept over the congregation.

But Robert was not there. He had now passed in reality through the gate of DEATH into ETERNITY. He was absent from the church on earth: he was present with the church in heaven. He was absent from the body that had slipped beneath the waters of Dundee harbour. But he was present with the Lord.

Books for Further Reading

AUTOBIOGRAPHY OF GEORGE MÜLLER
compiled by G. FRED BERGIN

GEORGE MÜLLER OF BRISTOL
DR. A. T. PIERSON
Pickering and Inglis Ltd, 29 Ludgate Hill, London

BY SEARCHING
ISOBEL KUHN

IN THE ARENA
ISOBEL KUHN

ONE VISION ONLY
CAROLYN CANFIELD
Overseas Missionary Fellowship, Newington Green, London
N16 9QD

BILLY BRAY, THE KING'S SON
F. W. BOURNE, Reprinted 1975
Epworth Press, now Methodist Publishing House, Wellington Road,
Wimbledon, London SW19 8EU

DAVID BRAINERD, HIS LIFE AND DIARY
edited by JONATHAN EDWARDS
The Tyndale Series of Great Biographies
Moody Press, The Moody Bible Institute, Chicago
and in *The Works of Jonathan Edwards*, vol. 2, Banner of Truth
Trust, 1975

ROBERT ANNAN
JOHN MACPHERSON (out of print)